ESSENTIAL COMMUNICATION STRATEGIES FOR SCIENTISTS, ENGINEERS, AND TECHNOLOGY PROFESSIONALS

Second Edition

HERBERT L. HIRSCH

Hirsch Engineering and Communications, Inc.
Vandalia, OH

IEEE PRESS

A JOHN WILEY & SONS, INC., PUBLICATION

Published by John Wiley & Sons, Inc., Hoboken, New Jersey.
Published simultaneously in Canada.

For general information on our other products and services please contact our Customer Care Department within the U.S. at 877-762-2974, outside the U.S. at 317-572-3993 or fax 317-572-4002.

Wiley also publishes its books in a variety of electronic formats. Some content that appears in print, however, may not be available in electronic format.

Library of Congress Cataloging-in-Publication Data Is Available

ISBN 0-471-27317-1

Printed in the United States of America.

10 9 8 7 6 5 4 3 2 1

ESSENTIAL
COMMUNICATION
STRATEGIES FOR
SCIENTISTS, ENGINEERS,
AND TECHNOLOGY
PROFESSIONALS

Second Edition

To my wife and best friend,
Susan Diane Hirsch
for her patience and support
through all these writing projects

CONTENTS

CONTENTS

CONTENTS

CONTENTS

PREFACE

The first edition of this book was published in 2000 as *The Essence of Technical Communication for Engineers*. The idea behind it was to provide effective communication strategies for technical people such as engineers to employ in the course of their careers. It included proven and reliable tricks and techniques for writing, presenting ideas, and participating in meetings; basically covering all kinds of communication situations a technologist was likely to encounter.

After the original edition appeared, it became apparent that its contents were applicable to a much broader scope of professionals than the title implied. The tricks and techniques work just as well for scientists, architects, researchers, doctors, and others as they do for engineers. So the title of the first edition, "The Essence of Technical Communication *for Engineers*," was really too constrained and did not represent the book's true value across the breadth and depth of technologists.

For the second edition, we have done a lot more than simply change the title. The first three parts, which mirror the original edition in title and contents, have been modified to be more general, setting out the tricks and techniques in a context that all technical professionals, regardless of experience, discipline, or specialty, will relate to.

Here, for example, a medical researcher, mechanical designer, or computer scientist will find the information just as useful as an electrical engineer would. Also, a fourth major part with four additional chapters has been added to address what we call *cross-culture communication*. This part shows how we can apply the tricks and techniques to reach unfamiliar audiences or readers, as would a scientist addressing a group of investors or an architect writing for corporate executives. Technology is pervasive in our culture today, and every technologist needs to be able to both recognize and overcome communication culture gaps to effectively communicate with nontechnical audiences or readers. The fourth part of this edition explains exactly how to achieve this kind of communication.

I believe this second edition will serve the communication needs of many technologists, across myriad disciplines and specialty areas. Readers of the first edition will find useful new material in Part IV, and new readers will find the entire book a handy guide for effective communication in any circumstance. As in the first edition, I have kept the entire book succinct and easy to read, and have included many real-world examples. I hope you enjoy it.

Herbert L. Hirsch
Hirsch Engineering and Communications, Inc.
Vandalia, OH

PREFACE TO THE FIRST EDITION

"Us engineers don't need no English" was a common saying around undergraduate engineering circles in my bachelor's program days. It seemed to be true. After all, in our entire engineering program, we were only required to take a token composition course in our freshman year. We were learning so many more interesting, technical ways to express ourselves. Surely, if we required better training in communication, the university would have provided a more comprehensive treatment. So who needs it, anyway?

As it turned out *we did*! We engineers *did* need some English, and we weren't getting it. This was the late 1960s, and we were caught up in the wonders of marvelous technological changes. Semiconductors and integrated circuits were thrusting the old vacuum-tube technology aside. The notion of software technology and its associated disciplines were in their infancy. It was a truly exciting time to be a young, aspiring engineer, and the idea of setting some of the technology aside to gain communication skills seemed a radical departure from "the important stuff" to students and faculty alike.

Now, many years later, it is still a truly exciting time for a young engineer (and even for a few old ones). However, although engineering schools are now offering technical writing and communication courses, it appears that the prevailing attitude is still that technologists do not need to hone their communication skills.

Unfortunately, that attitude is a dead-end trap. Technology will always be on the move, and its current state will always be exciting to emerging engineers. If it were boring, it surely wouldn't be worth all the effort of an engineering education, right? But what about the future? A few (very few) technologists will be so brilliant that their employers will be happy to surround them with a covey of technical writers. The vast majority will spend their entire careers promoting themselves and their ideas to gain acceptance, better pay, career advancement, or even career changes toward management or technical marketing, for example. For that majority, communication skills may very well mean the difference between having a rewarding and well-compensated senior position and one slinging fast food down at the local burger joint.

This little book is designed to guide technologists in their quest for these communication skills. Purely and simply, it is about *writing, presenting ideas,* and *interacting effectively* in a technical environment. Its purpose is to provide simple, useful, and effective communication tools to make communication both pleasant and easy for the practicing technologist. I hope you enjoy it.

Herbert L. Hirsch
Hirsch Engineering and Communications, Inc.
Vandalia, OH

ACKNOWLEDGMENTS

Portions of the Preface were previously published in:
Herbert L. Hirsch. 1994. Technical Communications. *IEEE Potentials* 13 (2).
Portions of the Introduction and Chapters 4, 5, and 6 were previously published in:
Herbert L. Hirsch. 1995. The technical presentation. *IEEE Potentials* 14 (3).
The lyrics quoted in Chapter 2, reprinted by permission from the Hal Leonard Corporation,
are from:
The First Thing You Know
from PAINT YOUR WAGON
Lyrics by Alan Jay Lerner
Music by Frederick Lowe
Copyright (c) 1969 by Chappell & Co.
Copyright Renewed
International Copyright Secured All Rights Reserved

INTRODUCTION TO THE ART OF COMMUNICATION

I like little books, don't you? For one thing, little books are easy to carry around with you. You don't have to worry about whether or not they will fit into a suitcase—they just go right into your pocket or briefcase. For another, little books are actually used as books, and not for other purposes. Big books are used to press leaves, prop up computers, and as bookends for other big books, but little books just get to travel around with someone and actually be read, the really nice thing that's supposed to happen to a book.

Also, little books tend to contain succinct, powerful, easy-to-understand, and easy-to-use information. I have a couple of favorites. The *Tao Te Ching,* which many consider to be the definitive treatise on oriental philosophy, is just about 80 pages long. It only gets longer when translators feel compelled to rationalize their approach to the translation process. And *The Elements of Style,* Strunk and White's excellent guide to writing, is a mere ninety-some pages long. I also have some large books, most of which are on this or that scientific, engineering, mathematical, or technical subject. I read my copy of the *Tao* frequently and use my Strunk and White daily. The cat sleeps on my bookcase full of lengthy, large books. Enough said.

I decided to write this little book to communicate the notion of effective communication. We live in a very complex, technically oriented age. Advances in information handling, distribution, processing, and visualization have spawned a culture in which information is available to everyone. Sadly, however, effective communication—the very means by which that information may be understood and used by those who may benefit from it—is an increasingly disappearing art. In this book, my goal is to convince you that communication is both easy and fun. I plan to do this by giving you some nifty little tools to apply the art of communication to your particular technologies, specialties, or interests. I have no doubt that this will make you better, happier, and more effective in all your communication endeavors.

My own idea of effective communication was awakened during a presentation of a technical paper early in my career. The presentation started with a bang! Well, actually it was more of a *piinng, click, click, click,* sound that echoed throughout the auditorium. It was the top button of my jacket popping off, striking the microphone, and rattling around the podium. My briefer's notes might have muffled the sound somewhat, but they were back at the hotel room. Quickly pocketing the button and glancing at the projection screen, I saw that my first chart was both upside down and reversed, clearly indicating that the individual who was in charge of handling my charts was even more disorganized than I, which was not particularly comforting. After coaching this person (over the auditorium's public address system for the enjoyment of all) on properly orienting the charts, which seemed to take an eternity, I finally turned toward the audience. Good, I had their attention! From that point on, the presentation went quite well and the audience was both attentive and polite. (I think they felt sorry for me.)

Actually, I was not quite so nonchalant about the whole experience. This was my first presentation to a large audience, and I was nervous going in. I didn't need all these problems, but after the ordeal was over, I had learned a few things. First, it was obvious that more preparation would have been helpful. Checking to make sure my notes were ready and arriving early enough to coordinate with the person in charge of the charts would have made quite a difference. Second, I saw the value of getting the audience's attention early, although I imagined that there were better ways to do this. Third, I noted that the whole event was indeed a valuable lesson—a learning experience. Finally, this had been the most catastrophic presentation of my career, so I had nothing but better things to look forward to in the future.

Years later, reflecting on this experience, I realized that it had taught me the essentials of a successful technical presentation: planning, attitude, and execution. Better *planning* would have avoided most of the problems (although probably not the bouncing button). The *attitude* that it had been a learning experience was a positive one, and the opinion that there were better things to come was correct and healthy: it's best not to dwell on bad experiences, but to anticipate better ones. The ability to *execute* the presentation despite problems was a confidence builder.

More generally, planning, attitude, and execution are the attributes that form the foundation of any technical communication event, written or oral, formal or informal. In this book, we're going to look at the nuances and particulars of these foundational attributes as they apply to all types of communication. Of these three attributes, planning is the most critical, because it is the stimulus for the other two. Good planning builds a confident attitude, which, in turn, ensures successful execution of the communication, regardless of its particular form.

But before delving into the more specific aspects, let us consider the need for good communication skills. Obviously, communication is everywhere. It is the essence of our existence. It is the only means we have to interact with others, and interaction is the basis of our culture. Furthermore, communication is the tool by which we operate our entire socioeconomic system, which is capitalism. Let's face it, capitalism is now, and will continue to be, the dominant paradigm by which our world will operate in the foreseeable future. This is not because capitalism is necessarily better than other systems, but because it is competitively stronger.

In fact, debating whether or not some socioeconomic system is better than another is akin to pondering whether a tiger is better than a rabbit. When these two animals encounter one another, the issue of which is "better" never surfaces, because rabbits are better at munching clover and tigers are better at munching rabbits. So the tiger simply eats the rabbit and that is that. Socialism, some may argue, is more fair or noble than capitalism. A few diehards in the world may still actually believe in and practice communism. However, in a world economy wherein capitalism and other forms must compete, those who practice capitalism will always win, because capitalism rewards competitive success. Capitalism is the tiger and the rest are the rabbits—*munch, munch.*

Then, given that we are going to operate within a capitalistic culture, there is a very important point to be made: we are all salespeople. This is a concept that some find hard to swallow. I have known many engineers, scientists, or other technologists who actually disdain their marketing or sales colleagues. They seem to believe that "selling" is beneath their dignity. What they should realize is that they not only have been selling virtually all their lives but must continue to do so throughout their careers. When they decided on their technical career, they sold themselves to a university. Upon graduation, they sold themselves to an employer. Now, within that employ-

4

er's system, they must sell their ideas to colleagues, supervisors, and clients in order to fund their research interests, gain promotions, or make their company or university profitable or at least solvent, so that they may remain employed. Failure to do so results in selling themselves to another employer. If these folks consider selling beneath their dignity, they should consider the relative indignity of unemployment.

Now, if we accept the fact that we are all salespeople, what is the means by which we sell? Communication! Our communication skills permit us to *write* the winning proposal, successful résumé, or effective technical document. They enable us to prepare and conduct interesting *presentations* that appeal to our audiences. And they allow us to *interact* effectively with colleagues, clients, potential employers, or other benefactors. In fact, we may coarsely divide our communication endeavors into these three types: writing, presenting, and interacting. Accordingly, I have divided this book into three parts corresponding to these three types of communication: the written document (writing), the formal presentation (presenting), and the informal discussion (interacting). For each type, I describe how to successfully apply the critical attributes of planning, attitude, and execution.

So now you see that this little book has to do with applying the proper *planning, attitude,* and *execution* to the acts of *writing, presenting,* and *interacting.* But this is not the essence of the book, not the nifty little tools I promised you. Planning, attitude, and execution are simply the necessary attributes set in the context of the three types of communication, and if that were all this little book provided, it would also be of little value. Lots of books, in many sizes and shapes, cover these subjects.

This little book, however, offers something more valuable—the fact that you only have to understand three principles to become an effective communicator, and these are the essence of communication. Three principles—three nifty little tools—and you're done. And what are these three powerful, simple principles that form the essence of communication? They are *connection, flow,* and *reinforcement,* which are no more than simple common sense applied to communicating. So let's get acquainted with them:

- *Connection.* This simply means connecting what we *have* to what some reader, audience, or listener *needs* or *wants.* We have a point to make or an idea to convey, but that point or idea may not be something the recipients of our communication will immediately grasp as being relevant or interesting. Hence, it is up to us, as the communicators, to make the connection, and not leave it to the recipients to sort out.
- *Flow.* This means taking the recipients of our communication smoothly and effortlessly from what they need or want to what we have (and not vice versa). It is the mechanism of the connection and, ideally, to the recipient, it should be as enjoyable as a favorite easy chair, as comfortable as an old pair of shoes. Again, it is up to us to provide this degree of comfort within our flow.
- *Reinforcement.* This means providing the support for the elements within our flow. Reinforcement is the substance—the collective, supporting details that are the foundation for the connection—and it must convince the recipients that our flow will work. The easy chair must be sturdy and the comfortable shoes must have good soles. Once again, it is up to us to demonstrate this support.

I like to think of these principles as a railroad trip. If we want to get a passenger to a destination, we define the destination, put the passenger on a comfortable sleeper, and make sure that the rails are sound, the bridges are in good repair, and the tunnels are clear. Consequently, the passenger will expect to reach the destination and will simply sit back and enjoy the ride. (Yes, I know an airplane trip would be a more contemporary metaphor, but I

6

honestly can't conceive of just sitting back and enjoying an airplane ride.) Similarly, if we want to get a communication recipient to accept an idea, we define the idea in terms of the recipient's interest, provide a comfortable flow from his or her interest to our idea, and make sure that the supporting details for our idea are sound, in good repair, and clear. The recipient will therefore expect to find something of value in our idea and will sit back and "enjoy the ride"—the communication experience.

We've been speaking rather metaphorically in these definitions of our three principles, but the notion is simple and clear. We provide a *connection* for our communication material to the recipient's needs, take him or her smoothly and effortlessly through the *flow* of this connection, and provide solid *reinforcement* for our flow. We also do the proper planning and assume the correct attitude. Consequently, we execute the communication event successfully, regardless of whether it is an informal meeting, a formal presentation, or a written document.

So this is it in a nutshell, so to speak: three powerful principles (connection, flow, and reinforcement) that can be applied through three attributes (planning, attitude, and execution) to the three types of communication (writing, presenting, and interacting). Three sets of three things each to learn to be a successful communicator. It sounds like I am hung up on the number *three* doesn't it? Not really, but maybe we should have charged you *three* times as much for this book. Oh well, maybe by keeping it inexpensive it will reach *three* times as many people as a big, expensive book.

Getting back to the point of all this (lest I permit my own flow to diverge from the connection I am trying to make), my aim is simply to demonstrate how to apply the principles. These principles are the constant force behind all communication. Once mastered, they become a useful road map by which we can navigate any communication endeavor, regardless of type or technical particulars. Once familiar, they can render the preparation and conducting of the communication an easy and enjoyable experience. Once forgotten, you will have to read this book again, but that's okay, because it's a *little* book. Now, one by one, we will look at the three types of communication and learn how to apply these three essential principles—our tools—to each. The essence, the core, the very heart of the concept remains constant: *connection, flow,* and *reinforcement.* There really are no other issues in communication, only variations in type and situation, as I shall proceed to explain.

I

THE WRITTEN DOCUMENT— PROSE AND PANIC

In this part of the book, we will discuss the attributes of planning, attitude, and execution necessary to produce a successful document. I had a difficult time deciding on the order in which to present the three types of communication, so I tossed a three-sided coin, and the written document won. No, not really. Actually I thought we should begin with the most controllable situation, and then work toward the least controllable one. Let's face it: writing is definitely the most controllable. You never had a document talk back or challenge your opinion, did you? Also, since the element of unpredictability grows as control declines, we can build on methods that work in controlled situations to derive methods that work in unpredictable ones. This sounds terribly logical and well organized, doesn't it? If you would rather believe the coin-toss rationale, just scribble out the previous sentence. By the way, that's another nice thing about little books—you don't feel guilty about scribbling in them.

1

PLANNING THE DOCUMENT

There are a number of different kinds of documents, including technical (and other) subject papers, proposals, articles, and books, to name a few. So, if we are going to work our way through document planning within a single chapter in a little book, we had better find some common ground. What is the common factor among all documents? Yes, I know they are printed (or at least portrayed as such on a screen). Nice try—but that's not it. The common denominator among all documents is that they each tell a story.

I once made this point to a group I was addressing, and one individual in the crowd became quite confrontational:

"That's not right," he said, "I can think of lots of documents that do not tell a story." "Such as?" I queried.

"Such as technical specifications, or product descriptions," he replied.

"Really," I responded. "Why don't you describe some of the details of these 'storyless' documents? Maybe we can find a story hidden within the details."

"Well, I can't really recall the details," he admitted.

Right, and that's the whole point. You can indeed create a storyless document, and it will have precisely the effect on its readers as the one my friend in the audience remembered (or actually didn't remember): nobody will recall its contents. Storyless documents are like seedless fruit—for immediate consumption but nothing more beyond that. They are shallow, boring, useless, meaningless drivel—and that is being polite about it.

Given, then, that good documents tell stories, what do we know about a story, especially one that is effective, memorable, and convincing? The answer is easy: it has a beginning and an end, which are connected by a smoothly flowing rhetoric that is well supported by necessary facts and details. Well what do you know—connection, flow, and reinforcement! Now where have we heard about these principles before?

These principles are especially important in document planning, because the document must stand on its own. Unlike a presentation or discussion, the author will not be there to clarify or elaborate—unless it is such a brilliant piece of work that he or she gets to go on tour and autograph it at bookstores. What's there is there, and that's it. Now let's look at our three principles in more detail, in the context of document planning.

MAKING THE CONNECTION

Making the connection is paramount, and I cannot overemphasize this point. It is the basis for all other activities in planning or preparing the document. Making the connection is to a written document (or any form of communication) what glue is to a model airplane: without it everything will fall apart.

So how do we make the communication connection in planning our document? The answer is simple: we must understand our readers and what we want to tell them. Half of this notion is sometimes lost on us as technologists. We certainly understand our subject and want to tell someone about it, but we often fail to discern what readers may find interesting in the subject. This can result in writing that is both incomplete and confusing to readers, and approaches the whole issue from the wrong direction.

When making the connection, we do not start with our subject and then decide how to connect it to our readers. Rather, we start with our readers' needs or desires and decide how to connect our subject to them. This requires additional effort. We have to understand the readers' needs to decide how our subject may be properly connected. This means we may have to research our intended readership before deciding on the connection. It is always worthwhile. I have seen countless business, technical, book, and article proposals (including my own) turned down because they failed to make the connection. Editors and publishers know the importance of this connection, and that is why we have to describe our target audience when we write a proposal to publish something. Many writers do not know this, but now that you do, we can proceed with more particulars of the connection.

Given that we do our research and have a connection firmly in mind, how should we plan to present it? For example, let's say we are going to submit a technical paper to a medical symposium on immunization deficiency disorders, and we know that the medical professionals are simply dying to get their hands on anything that will strengthen patients' immune systems. Let's also assume that we have devised a genetic technique that we know will provide such strengthening, because we have absolutely tested it to death; we are microbiologists engaged in genome research and simply adore finding new things to do with genes.

A really great place to make the connection is the title of the work. That's pretty logical isn't it? It's the first thing someone will read. So what is a good title? Consider this:

"ADVANCED GENETIC RESEARCH: THE KEY TO
IMPROVING HUMAN IMMUNITY"

Oh no, a titling disaster! But it made the connection between immunity and genetic research, so what's the big deal? The big deal is that it did *not* make the connection *from* immunity *to* genetic research. The review panel takes one look at this title and says, "Terrific, another bunch of genome zealots trying to shove their stuff down our throats." A much better title would be

"IMPROVING HUMAN IMMUNITY THROUGH GENETIC RESEARCH"

Now this is better. This title gets the job done because it begins with the readers' interest (human immunity) and follows to the idea we are presenting (genetic methods). But this title is a little dull—sort of passive-voicey and not much of an attention-getter. We really need to think of something that catches the readers' interest as well as makes the connection. Consider this one:

"IMMUNITY ADVANCEMENTS THROUGH GENETICS (IMAGEN)"

Nifty—a veritable *coup d'état* in titling. We start with the needs (immunity), connect to the idea (genetics), even assert the benefit (advancements), and also form the acronym *IMAGEN* with some of the letters of the key words (IMmunity Advancements through GENetics). What more could we ask for? We made the connection and got ourselves an acronym that implies something will be achieved that one can only "imagine" (IMAGEN—we don't have to be too fussy about spelling things correctly when crafting an acronym). The acronym is helpful because we will be able to refer to the technique simply as IMAGEN throughout the work, thus avoiding repetitions of a long, boring description, and giving the technique a hopeful and optimistic flavor. The important point is that we made the connection *from* the readers' interest *to* our idea, and not the other way around.

ESTABLISHING THE FLOW

Where else do we make the connection in a document? All over the place, such as in prefaces, introductions, or summary remarks in sections or chapters, but we do this in a logical, flowing manner. The purpose of the flow is to implement the connection. As I said earlier, it is the mechanism of the connection. Documents do differ in format, and some, such as proposals, may have a very rigid format to which we must adhere. So what? Flow is not format. Rather, flow is the way we achieve the connection, using a format as the structural framework.

Let's consider an example of flow planning. In a technical paper or maybe a proposal, we would generally follow a sequence of stating the problem, describing our research objectives, discussing our approach, presenting the actual or expected results, and giving a summary. Given this general format, the flow among major sections of the document would look something like this:

1. *The Problem*—We assert the readers' needs or interest, add sufficient details to convince readers we understand the problem, and briefly summarize the benefit of our solution. This tells the readers we are interested in and knowledgable of their needs and have something of value to offer. Note the immediate presentation of the connection (*from* their problem *to* our solution)? This will stimulate readers to continue reading for more details.
2. *Research Objectives*—We describe our objectives and explain how they will serve to solve the problem. Do you see the beginnings of a flow here? (Achieve the objectives to solve the problem.)
3. *Approach*—We describe how our approach (tasks, techniques, and results) was designed to achieve the objectives. The flow continues. (The approach was designed to produce results to achieve the objectives to solve the problem.)

4. *Results*—We elaborate on our results, making sure we "close the loop." That is, we describe how these results pertain to solving the problem. "Flow, flow, flow your boat. . . ." (Results from the approach *did* or *should* achieve the objectives to solve the problem.)
5. *Summary*—We simply remind readers that our understanding of the problem led to the proper objectives and that we (1) designed an approach to (2) produce results to (3) achieve those objectives. *Return of the flow*—the sequel.

If we look at the entire notion of flow, presented in the context of this example, we see that everything works to-

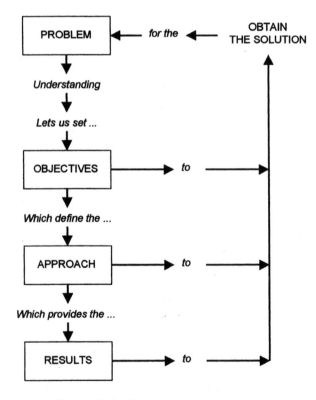

Figure 1.1 Flow in a Document.

gether to make the connection. Figure 1.1 is a type of flow chart that illustrates this concept. (If we have flow, I guess we had better be able to draw a flow chart, hadn't we?)

In our specific example, it is a *problem–solution* connection, but more generally, it is a type of *audience interest–our subject* connection we are implementing through our flow. Variations on this theme will naturally occur as a consequence of different documents, subject matter, or readership. But the fundamental principle remains constant: take the readers through the connection in an easy flowing and comfortable manner, and continually reassert the connection. In the introduction to each of the flow format sections, we would write some text that reminds the readers how that particular section relates to the connection, and probably reassert the connection in each section's summary or conclusive remarks. Now, in the context of planning, what is the best way to positively ensure a good flow?

The best way, in fact the only way, is to write a script for the document. I like to use the term *script* because, to me, it implies a more dynamic form of planning than a mere outline, such as for a play. We certainly want structure, but we also want a little action, a little life in the document. We're telling a story here, and what better way to plan it than to script it? And what is the difference between a script and an outline? The outline simply defines the structure of a document (what goes where). A script takes this structure and embellishes it with the points to be made in the connecting text to ensure the flow. It specifies precisely what we are going to write but in a more dynamic manner.

When we write a script for a document, we start with a flow diagram, such as the one in Figure 1.1, and an outline. Then we list the points we need to make in each section to make sure the flow is achieved as our first script. Next, we go ahead and actually write introductions, summaries, transitional phrases, and so forth, until we basically have all the "glue words" in place. This is our second

17

script, with elaborated flow points. At this juncture, the document can be tested for cohesive flow by simply reading what is there and assuming that any listed points not yet elaborated will indeed be elaborated. Let's look at an example of this progression from outline through scripts.

Assume that we are neural network experts writing a technical paper for a medical trade journal called "Medical Imaging with Neural Networks for Improved Effectiveness (MINNIE)." The title once again satisfies our criteria of connecting from the audience's needs (medical imaging) to our approach (neural networks). First of all, we'll create an outline, and then we'll develop the first script for the abstract and the first two sections of the flow format—The Problem Statement and Research Objectives—and compare them. To begin, the outline might appear as follows:

OUTLINE

**Medical Imaging with Neural Networks
for Improved Effectiveness (MINNIE)**

    Abstract
1.0 The Problem
1.1 A Critical Problem in Medical Imaging
1.2 A Potential Neural-Network Solution
1.3 Problem Summary
2.0 Research Objectives
2.1 Objective 1: Assess the Capability of Existing Neural Networks
2.2 Objective 2: Modify the Neural Networks to Enhance the Imagery—the MINNIE System
2.3 Objective 3: Test the Modified Neural Networks
2.4 Objective 4: Analyze the Results
2.5 Objectives Summary

Now there's absolutely nothing wrong with this outline. It describes what is to be written and where these parts should be. But before we actually start writing, we must settle on what our connection is going to assert and how our flow is going to work. Now comes the first script, which embeds particular points (P1, P2, and so forth) to be made. Continuing this example, let's take a look at the first script we might prepare for the MINNIE paper:

FIRST SCRIPT

Medical Imaging with Neural Networks or Improved Effectiveness (MINNIE)

Abstract
P1: Briefly describe the problem to be solved.
P2: Preview how MINNIE will solve it.
P3: Overview the contents of the paper.
P4: Lead-in to Problem section.
1.0 The Problem
P1: Introduce and overview the section.
    1.1 A Critical Problem in Medical Imaging
P1: Assert the critical problem—interpolating hidden details among scanned images.
P2: Define why it is critical.
P3: Describe benefits of a solution.
    1.2 A Potential Neural-Network Solution
P1: Briefly overview how neural networks can solve the problem.
P2: Cite an analogous problem already solved by neural networks.
    1.3 Problem Summary
P1: Summarize problem criticality and likelihood of success with this technique.
P2: Lead-in to Objectives section.
2.0 Research Objectives
P1: Introduce and overview the section.
    2.1 Objective 1: Assess the Capability of Existing Neural Networks
P1: Describe particular aspects to be assessed.
    2.2 Objective 2: Modify the Neural Networks to Enhance the Imagery—the MINNIE System

P1: Describe anticipated modifications to be made.

2.3   Objective 3: Test the Modified Neural Networks

P1: Describe tests to be performed.

2.4   Objective 4: Analyze the Results

P1: Describe analysis of results to be performed.

2.5   Objectives Summary

P1: Summarize in the context of objectives properly addressing the problem.

P2: Lead-in to Approach section.

As I discussed earlier, this is our nonelaborated script, containing the flow points as well as the technical points we need to make to produce the document we desire. Now, let's convert these flow points in the Abstract and Section 1.0 into text, thus creating this portion of our second script, with elaborated flow points and still unelaborated technical points. For the purpose of this example, I am making certain assumptions regarding the problem and solution purely for example's sake, which may or may not be technically correct. (This is a writing example, not a technically perfect, critically acclaimed neural-network discussion.) In this example, I indicate the points that have been elaborated in brackets.

SECOND SCRIPT

Medical Imaging with Neural Networks for Improved Effectiveness (MINNIE)

Abstract

A critical problem plaguing the medical imaging community is the inability to correctly and rapidly interpolate imagery among scanned images. Correctness is of the utmost importance, because the physician's interpretation of the imagery will guide diagnosis and subsequent treatment. Speed is also important, especially in cases in which the patient is in a life-threatening situation, and rapid, immediate diagnosis and action are required. [P1, Abstract]

Our MINNIE technique offers a unique approach to obtaining both the accuracy and speed required to satisfy the needs of the medical imaging community. In this paper, we describe how our technique can satisfy these critical, demanding, and often conflicting needs. [P2, Abstract]

This paper is a complete yet concise picture of our research and its results. We begin with a discussion of the medical imaging problem, concentrating on the aspect of critical accuracy versus speed. Next, we describe our research objectives, which were designed to focus our effort on obtaining a solution to this problem. Then, we describe our approach to achieving these objectives, which includes the systemic modification and application of existing neural-network technologies to this problem. Finally, we present our research results, in the context of solving this critical problem of accuracy versus speed of interscan interpolation in medical imaging. [P3, Abstract] Having set the stage with this overview, we will now proceed to describe the problem we tackled. [P4, Abstract]

1.0 The Problem

In this section, we describe our research problem. We begin with an overview of what makes interpolating the details among scanned images so difficult. Here, we also describe the benefits of solving this problem: why the solution is critical to the medical imaging community. Next, we briefly overview our neural-network solution, citing analogous problems already solved with this technique. Finally, we summarize, in the context of the degree of success, what we expected when we embarked on this research. [P1, Section 1.0]

1.1   A Critical Problem in Medical Imaging

P1:   Assert the critical problem—interpolating hidden details among scanned images.

P2:   Define why it is critical.

P3:   Describe benefits of a solution.

1.2   A Potential Neural-Network Solution

P1: Briefly overview how neural networks can solve the problem.

P2: Cite an analogous problem already solved by neural networks.

1.3 Problem Summary

P1: Summarize problem criticality and likelihood of success with this technique.

Having described our problem, the benefits of solving it, and our research expectations when we began this effort, we set the stage for describing our research. Our next step was to assert certain, specific objectives for our investigations into MINNIE. We next present these objectives. [P2, Section 1.3]

Note the smooth transition we are achieving. As we go from outline to script to second script, we move from pure structure to unelaborated content to semielaborated content, with a powerful result. After the flow points are elaborated, the writer elaborating the technical points has two goals: to make them technically correct (as usual) and to fit them into the flow created by the script. For example, look at the introductory paragraph for Section 1.0. It defines the context of the technical points required for Sections 1.1, 1.2, and 1.3. Here, we have achieved flow and also provided instructions for the technical writers, all in the same form—no need for separate writers' instructions. This is especially useful when multiple writers are involved, because it keeps them in the flow (or keeps the train on the tracks, to return to the earlier metaphor). The integrating author or editor will find the contributions from multiple writers much easier to fit into the whole piece, which will instantly have the cohesiveness often so hard to achieve.

Now is a good time to make another important point. We can design the entire document, make the connection, establish the flow, and even produce a semielaborated document framework without inserting one single technical detail. In fact, I have found that a good writer, free from the burdens of specific technical understanding, will often produce a better script than expert technologists, who may be tempted to bend the readers' needs to suit their technology. By establishing this script and flow, the technical details are forced to fit into a proper framework, as I discuss next.

PROVIDING THE REINFORCEMENT

Once we have articulated the connection and flow, in the form of a semielaborated script, we are ready to insert the technical nuances. Now it's time to chase the cat off the large books and bring some solid technical matter into play. I call these critical technical points *reinforcement* because they are the real foundation of what we are writing. We established the connection and flow in the readers' point of view, to keep them interested. But even the most interested readers will quickly tire of a shallow and unsupported dissertation.

We plan the reinforcement by adding the particular technical points to any nonelaborated flow points left within the script. As I just mentioned, these flow points, along with the flow elaboration, serve to focus the technical writings. Using this technique, we will not have disparate, out-of-context technical dissertations. As long as the technical contributors participate in the planning, and subsequently make their points, the document will be cohesive, interesting, and to the point. It will tell the story of a connection from the readers' needs to an idea in a fluid and focused manner, making the key technical points along the way. Readers will feel fulfilled, satisfied, and even entertained if our writing skills are good. It will be a successful document, regardless of its specific subject matter.

ZERO-TIME PLANNING

Our discussions to this point speak of the essentials of document planning, assuming we have time to carry them out. But what about the panic state? In other words, how on earth do we plan a document when some sage (usually someone who has a certain degree of influence or authority over us and does not do his or her own planning very well) demands a document and there is no time for planning? My advice here is simple: tell them to take a hike (do it mentally—it will make you feel better) and then assess your situation and resources. Maybe you can derive this document from a similar one, or paste together some existing documents, providing you have the appropriate permissions to use them for this purpose. Having done the planning or scripting for these existing works, you may visualize ways to write some additional "glue words" and at least form some semblance of cohesiveness.

Above all, don't skip the planning altogether. Unplanned documents are pure chaos. You would, in most cases, be better off not producing the document at all than assembling or writing it unplanned. However, this point is almost always lost on some folks who procrastinate and then demand instant results. Schedule your time, do your best, and most important, make sure the person who requested the document on such an unrealistic schedule knows what to expect. Excellent writing is a craft. It is a communication art form not unlike painting; rushing will result in a paint-by-the-numbers effect, whereas allowing time for the planning as well as the painting itself will certainly result in a thing of beauty, and occasionally a Rembrandt. The same goes for writing.

Now that we have looked at the aspects of planning, it is time for us to start thinking about attitude, which is what a good communicator needs to cultivate before actually starting to write. We'll do just that in the next chapter.

2

ACQUIRING A HEALTHY WRITING ATTITUDE

In this chapter, we will look into how we may establish the best attitude for writing our material. I differ somewhat from the conventional format here, because I present both method and philosophy. A more conventional approach would be to assert the three attributes of successful communication as planning, *preparation* (instead of attitude), and execution. In my opinion, however, preparation is not an attribute. It is a building block that, along with anticipation and enthusiasm, serves to produce the kind of *attitude* that will permit us to write excellent documents. Hence, I now present the philosophy and method within these building blocks necessary to acquire the right attitude.

PREPARING TO WRITE

Preparing to write is, in essence, just like preparing to do anything else; it is both physical and mental. The physical part is easy. We simply need to get our writing materials together. So we gather up our references, get a nice clean disk and a few snacks (in case we get on a roll and need to forge ahead—we don't want to run out of energy), and basically anything we need or want to make our writing environment comfortable. If you like neatness, make it neat. If you like clutter, clutter it up really well. Just make it the way you want it. The mental part may not be so easy, but it can be. We gather up our mental facilities and a nice clean attitude, and away we go. Sounds simple, doesn't it? Well, of course it does, *because it is.*

My goal here is not to provide you with a bunch of attitude-enhancing trickery. There are lots of books (mostly big ones) full of those things. These big books will tell you how to sit, eat, exercise, even adjust your love life to become properly motivated. They are good leaf pressers and bookends, all of them. Instead, I am going to show you that you are already motivated. Your train is on the tracks and moving, and all you have to do is jump on board.

Let's take a look at why we are motivated and have the right attitude to start writing. At this point, we have created a script for our piece, so we know exactly what we are going to write. Furthermore, we have gathered up all our writing materials, so we know we have the means to write it. We can be enthusiastic. We have everything together. We're like a train coming down the mountain. (That train metaphor is getting a little old. I'll try to think of something new for the next chapter.) So let's get going!

ANTICIPATING THE READERS' NEEDS

Actually, let's *not* get going, at least not right away. Let's put the snacks back into the refrigerator and wait a while. Let's savor the feeling of readiness and enthusiasm, so we don't lose it, and think a bit about who we are writing this work for, as we savor it.

Believe it or not, I actually follow my own advice, unlike certain evangelists and politicians. I created an outline for this chapter and wrote a script. Then I got my materials together, got my environment the way I like it (actually, because I always do this type of writing in my home office, it's always ready—a beautiful assimilation of odds and ends, a virtual masterpiece of clutter), and began to feel really good about writing this chapter. That was a few weeks ago, and I have been feeling good about it ever since.

Over those weeks, I have also done a lot of other things—worked for some clients, enjoyed activities with my family, chopped firewood, and basically went about my life. However, in the back of my mind, I was thinking about you—the reader I wanted to reach with this chapter. I thought about your needs and motivations, and how I might pose this material so that you would enjoy reading it and gain something from it. Ideas, phrases, words, and basically everything you are now reading went through my head at one time or another. Finally, today, I woke up and thought to myself: "This is a fine day to write Chapter 2." So I did, and here it is.

The point here is that we get enthusiastic about writing something based on our physical preparation, and then we let the readers' needs well up within us as we are savoring that fine enthusiasm we have wrought. It works every time, and I honestly can't tell you why. It simply does. Try it yourself. Get your script done, get your stuff together, get happy about it, and think about the nice thing you will do for your readers. As you savor this, and your ideas start coming, your enthusiasm will mount, and eventually you will feel so compelled to start writing, you may even forget about the snacks. Actually, if you savor the work long enough, the snacks may be a bit stale and not worth having anyway. At any rate, this feeling about satisfying the readers' needs is both necessary and is itself an enthusiasm builder.

ENTHUSIASM: ENJOYING IT AND
AVOIDING WRITER'S BLOCK

At this point, if we have done the physical preparation, savored our enthusiasm, and thoughtfully worked out how to satisfy our readers, our attitude is just about at its peak. The single extra ingredient we need, to push us into the writing itself, is knowing we are going to enjoy it. And why shouldn't we enjoy it? We've prepared, let the right time come along, and now all we have to do is *do it.*

However, at this juncture, some folks will be overcome by a particular type of nervousness. There is even a term for it—*writer's block*—which defines a condition in which we have all we need to write but just can't seem to get going. Again, there are many volumes of expert advice and tricks for escaping the clutches of this dreaded nemesis. And, of course, these are mostly large books (and you already know what I think of them) because there is always a ready market for solutions to problems we can solve by ourselves. The fact is, what we call writer's block is simply an artifact of forcing ourselves to write before we have finished our savoring process. If we merely wait a while, and let the ideas come while our enthusiasm is high, this problem simply cannot exist. But what if we have a schedule to meet? I'll talk about that in the next section. For now, we're talking about having fun writing things, not about schedules.

I think writing is one of the most enjoyable aspects of technical endeavors for one simple reason—freedom. The whole notion is stated perfectly in a passage from a musical by Lerner and Loewe called *Paint Your Wagon.* Let me explain my point.

The show is about the adventures and misadventures of some pioneers and gold miners in old California. The lead character, one Ben Rumson, is a rugged mountain man who has little use for the encroachment of civilization. His point of view is wonderfully summarized in a few lines from a song called "The First Thing You Know," which go like this:

28

> They civilize left and they civilize right,
> 'Til nothing is left and nothing is right.
> They civilize freedom 'til no-one is free,
> No-one except, by coincidence, me.

We can easily find the analogy in our structured, disciplined business and technology culture of today:

> They organize left and they discipline right,
> 'Til nothing is left and nothing is right.
> They structure our work 'til no-one is free,
> No-one except, by coincidence, *me*.

If we think of ourselves as the persona of the *me* in the second passage, we can really enjoy writing. The fact of the matter is that the whole world has become so structured and disciplined in its endeavors that there is very little freedom left in technology. It's all rules, rules, and more rules. Writing is an escape for the creative person, and I think that there is a lot of creativity in everyone, just aching to get out and do something great.

When we write, we are subject only to the rules of format, grammar, and good communication. Within these bounds, we can do anything we like. We can use railroad metaphors, cite passages from musicals, talk about big and little books, and basically just have a good time with the whole thing. Just try to find any similar freedom in, for instance, an object-oriented design paradigm. Don't try for long though, because you won't find it and just thinking about it will frustrate you. We can enjoy the creative act of effective writing as one of the few remaining freedoms in technology. So let's do it.

There is a danger, though. Once you get into the fun and freedom afforded by creative writing, you may not want to go back to doing technology things. It happened to me, and it can happen to you; but let me tell you, it's not all bad. These days, I do mostly technical writing for a living, and I enjoy it. Then, for recreation, I do science and engineering the way I want to, and not according to some set of rules. Occasionally, when I discover something nifty in my technical tinkerings, I write a book or an article about it, and it's a pleasure.

In summary, knowing you are going to enjoy your writing and preparing and anticipating the readers' needs are the keys to a good attitude. Regardless of your environment, and whether or not you ascribe to structure and rules, these elements are the essence of the matter. Now, having established these attributes of a good writing attitude, let's talk about how your situation may conspire to try and wreck that attitude, and what to do about it.

ZERO-PLANNING ATTITUDE ADJUSTMENTS: THEIRS, NOT OURS!

Would you take a cake out of the oven when it was half baked and try to eat it? No. Would you move into a new house before it was finished? No. Would some people ask you to write something in such a hurry you could not do it properly? Yes, of course they would, because some folks specialize in the half baked and the unfinished. So what shall we do about this?

Well, first of all, How important is it to you to work for these people? I'm serious here, folks. If you are working within an organization that is so overbearing, rigid, and unwilling to listen to common sense that unreasonable time constraints will be a continual problem, go find another job. If, however, this problem occurs only occasionally, or you believe the folks you work with will actually listen to you, there are a couple of things you can do.

First, you can try to educate them. Give them the idea that they basically get what they pay for, in both money and schedule. If they constrain a writer to an unrealistic schedule, they will get an inferior product. What if Leonardo da Vinci had been hired as an employee and then tasked to paint the Mona Lisa? You can just picture him meeting with his supervisor:

"Leo, you're behind schedule and over budget. You need to get this thing finished by Friday."

"Sorry, boss, but I just can't get the smile right. I need some more time."

"No can do, Leo. Business is business, so we're taking you off the project. In fact, we're going to have to let you go. Sorry, but we just can't tolerate employees who will not work within our schedules and budgets. We'll get someone down in the drafting department to finish the smile. It can't be a very big deal to do that."

So they get a painting with Mona Lisa's face and a smile that could stampede a herd of elephants. They probably retitle it "Happy Mona" or something equally insipid, as illustrated in Figure 2.1, and it winds up just the way they made it—a piece of junk.

Figure 2.1   Happy Mona. Drawing by Alan Hirsch.

Second, you can show examples of the successful projects that were allowed to proceed according to a reasonable schedule and point out the rush jobs that produced garbage. You will find these successes and failures easily; they exist in every organization. Encourage those you write for to consider the facts and make the right decision.

After all your efforts to educate and reason with these people, what if they decide that they *still* want stuff produced so quickly and cheaply that it can't be any good? Do you still want to work for them? It's your decision. Life will be much easier if you face the fact that you shouldn't try to change these people. There's an old saying: "You can't teach a pig to sing. No matter how hard you try, it never sounds very good, and it upsets the pig." You also can't teach some people to be good planners and organizers of work. Maybe these folks are perfectly content to produce junk, simply because that is what they can sell. After all, as I pointed out in Chapter 1, we are fundamentally capitalists, and the name of the game is often "make it cheap and sell it for what you can get." In either case, arguing or debating with such people is futile. Besides, why should you get frustrated just because some folks are unreasonable? They're not your children. You are not responsible for instilling proper values or behavior in them, so leave them alone.

You can also make life easier by detaching yourself from the process somewhat. You've heard of an out-of-body experience? In case you haven't, it's a condition in which the spirit departs the body for a little excursion and goes merrily off on its own for a while. Do something similar. Let your spirit wander out and enjoy some entertaining daydreaming. Actually, it's easy to do this. Since these folks are not looking for exceptional quality (by a long shot), just roll out the words, don't worry about producing really high quality writing (since they don't expect it), and meet the schedules and budgets (*and by all means, decline the byline*). Actually, with a little practice, you can perfect almost a dual consciousness in these situations.

32

You can grind out the product almost automatically and think about something enjoyable at the same time. In fact, I got a lot of ideas for this book while I was writing a piece on the benefits of structured design techniques (truly mindless work, because it is at least a paradox if not a blatant contradiction to use *benefit* and *structured design* in the same sentence). If you really want to do creative writing, do it on the side. Write some articles, papers, or anything you like, and enjoy it.

In this manner, you accomplish two things. First, you keep the folks you write for pacified. Second, you get to have some fun and improve your skills, which allows you to maintain a positive attitude. When you improve your skills sufficiently, you can find some other folks to work for or start freelancing. If you are truly creative and enjoy writing, you will not be happy writing in a pacify-the-unreasonable style for very long.

Well, we've come to the end of Chapter 2. Now you see how to develop and keep an enthusiastic, or at least fairly positive, attitude. Next, in Chapter 3, we are going to look at how to actually go about the writing task itself, to produce the document. But before I write it, I think I'll fiddle around with some other things for a while. I've got some nifty stuff for Chapter 3, and I want to make it just right for you. Besides, I promised you a new metaphor for the next chapter (goodbye, train), and I need to think of one.

3

PRODUCING THE DOCUMENT

I have only two things to talk about in this chapter: simplicity and isolation. See, everything in this little book doesn't come in *threes*. Once we have done our planning and cultivated our attitude, we are ready to start writing. Now, in actually doing the writing, we use simple tools to get the job done, isolate ourselves from things that would interrupt us, and start pounding out the words. By following these ideas, we can get the job done posthaste, although still probably not fast enough for some of the wizards who set the schedules. Oh well, let's not get hung up on that issue—at least not yet. Let's look at this chapter's two ideas.

SIMPLICITY: WHY OVERCOMPLICATE THE TASK?

We need to strive for simplicity. Simple, succinct, to-the-point prose is powerful and effective. Long, wordy, elaborate dissertation is not. Similarly, fast, easy, helpful tools are powerful, whereas elaborate, complicated ones are not. We need simplicity in prose and in tools to get the job done right, and the first step is getting the tools.

In this day and age, if you are going to write anything, you are probably going to use a word processor. If you are still using a typewriter, good for you! You have already achieved simplicity in your tools. Skip over this part and go to the section on isolation. In fact, if you use a typewriter, you are probably already pretty well isolated, so head for the next chapter. For the rest of us, let's take a short look at word processors. Now I promised that this would not be a book on mechanics, and I'm not jumping ship here (a new metaphor, just like I promised). I am not going to get into the nuances of how to use a word processor. Rather, we are going to take a look at how to get a word processor that can actually be used.

The original notion of word processing was simple. We could use the computer's ability to add, delete, and organize things to eliminate all the problems with whiting out errors, gluing in drawings, and so forth. By moving from a physical construction to an electronic construction, we could become more efficient and productive. This was a good idea; we could do all the necessary tasks we always did with greater efficiency, and more. Doing the necessary things was fine, but when word processor developers moved into the "and more" realm, they opened a Pandora's box. In fact, had Pandora been a regular user of one of the elaborate word processors of today, her opening the box would have seemed pale by comparison. In fact, she probably would not have noticed the ramifications of opening the box at all.

Let's critique word processors. What do we want to do when we activate our word processor? We want to write something. What do we need in order to write something? A clear screen and control over the same things we had control over with a typewriter—tabs, margins, line spacing, columns, and typeface (font). What else can word processors do for us that is useful? They can give us alternative and mixed fonts and type sizes, let us paste in objects electronically, check our spelling, and do a few special things with our characters, such as set italics, boldface, underlines, superscripts, and subscripts. Now, what can word processors do for us that is useless? Everything else they do while trying to be more like desktop publishers. Finally, what can word processors do for us that goes beyond useless and is absolutely frustrating? Make us wade through all the useless stuff, or customize their silly system, just to get to the few simple, useful features that are all we needed in the first place.

I have a good word processor. In fact, it's an excellent word processor. It's also a very simple word processor. I knew it would be simple when I bought it, because it only cost $16. Actually, that's an estimate because it was part of the Microsoft Works package, which also included a spreadsheet and a database, and cost about $50. So I figure all three are about equal in complexity (actually, simplicity), and $16 is about one third of $50. By the way, the Works spreadsheet and database are also excellent ones for the same reason—simplicity. The three applications in this package are in fact simplified abstractions of Microsoft's more elaborate software.

Microsoft has my eternal gratitude. It created my highly useful word processor by simplifying Word, its overly complicated $120 word processor (part of the $480 Microsoft Office suite, which contains three other overly complicated applications). I would have gladly paid $120 for the simple and easy-to-use Works word processor, but Microsoft only wanted $16. I occasionally use Word because it is the word processor of choice among my clients, but I usually write in Works and then translate it to Word as the last step before delivering or printing the final document. To me, Word is kind of a printer driver or final document packager, and certainly not something I would use for writing extensively. However, Microsoft sells thousands of copies of Word to thousands of people, along with the rest of the Office Suite, for about $480. If you want to use Word, or any similarly complicated word processor, my advice is to get into the formatting and options menus and disable everything that is automatic, such as automatic bulleting, numbering, indenting, and so forth. This will return it to the state it was in a few versions ago, when it was a truly useful tool. Nothing makes me happier than to see a tab-indexed set of options with all of them turned off. Then I know the word processor will be doing what I want it to do and not what some designer of the silly thing thought I might want to do. Stay in charge of your writing.

When I open my word processor, I see a clear, clean screen and the few simple functions I need. When you open your word processor, this is what you want to see, too. The writing may be complex and the subject may be complicated. So use the simple tools that will let you get right to the writing task without adding their own complexity. Leave the fancy stuff to the production people. Simplify. Thoreau was right.

ISOLATION: GET AWAY FROM THE INTERRUPTIONS

Thoreau had a pretty good idea about eliminating distractions, too: go live in a small cabin by a pond. It would probably work just fine, but most of us can't get quite that isolated and still function. However, the notion is a valid one. You simply can't concentrate on writing if you allow yourself to be interrupted all the time, and we all have the power to eliminate these interruptions.

First of all, we need to separate ourselves physically from interruptions. This may or may not be easy, depending on the circumstances. If you can, lock yourself up in your office and make it clear to your coworkers that you are writing and cannot be disturbed. If this does not work, or if you work in one of today's honeycombs of cubicles, see if you can locate another spot, a hiding place so to speak, where you can be left alone to concentrate. If you need some of your office resources, however, moving away from distractions may be inconvenient, and you will have to try the lockout method.

One reason the lockout method does not work for some people is that they do not do it seriously. They probably say something like, "I am going to be writing now, so please do not disturb me for a while." Polite, but probably ineffective. It's better to say, "I am going to be writing now and anyone who interrupts me will bear the responsibility for any missed deadlines or poor-quality writing." Even better, when the first person tries to interrupt, for any reason, do something dramatic. A good tactic is to keep a useless disk in your disk drive (this is just a prop; you're actually working off the hard drive). Then when an inconsiderate coworker sticks his or her head in your door, you bite it off—figuratively at least. First, slam your hands down on the desk. Next, yank the dummy disk out of the disk drive and sling it hard into the wastebasket so it really makes a *clang*! Then glare directly into the person's face and with teeth clenched say, "What is it?" At this point, you'll usually get some lame excuse or unimportant drivel. Then simply say, "I'll get back to you," keep those teeth clenched, turn around, stare at your screen, and don't move until the person leaves.

To complete the gambit, you need to do some follow-up. Later on, seek out the interrupter, act as if nothing happened, be just as nice and pleasant as you can be, and ask what it was he or she wanted earlier. If the person asks about the previous encounter, just say, "Oh, that's just me when I am writing, a bit temperamental I guess," and refuse to elaborate further. Pretty soon, after you do this a few times, you'll get the reputation of someone who should not be interrupted. You'll have fewer interruptions, and your writing will have the potential to be truly effective.

I use the word *potential* here because you still have another form of interruption to overcome: the electronic interruption. There are lots of these, in many forms. Maybe there is an office paging system, or perhaps one of those pesky little e-mail systems that is compelled to beep at you just because you have new mail. Interestingly, the mailbox at the end of my driveway never beeps at me. Good thing, too, because if it did it would have an encounter with my axe. Anyhow, we can turn off pagers, disable e-mail beepers, and so forth, but we still have a formidable enemy—the telephone.

When you get right down to it, the telephone is unquestionably the mother of all interrupters. It even interrupts itself: little sounds signal you, after you have already been interrupted by one call, that another call is waiting to interrupt the first one! However, improvements in telephone technology have given us an edge. Am I talking about voice mail? Call waiting? Call forwarding? Heck, no. I am talking about the plug-in telephone. Just unplug it. Simple.

I think the plug-in telephone is the most valuable achievement in telephone technology of our time. It used to be that if you wanted privacy, you had to unwire the telephone, or leave the handset off the hook. The latter tactic sometimes precipitated an annoying buzz or beep designed to alert you that the handset was off the hook. (Of course it was off the hook—you purposely took it off!) Either way, it was rather inconvenient. But with the plug-in telephone, all you have to do is unplug it. It's great— just like it doesn't exist at all—and you can really get a lot of writing done. Then, later, when you are ready to let the clutter through, you can just plug the telephone back in. Try it. It's one of the most satisfying feelings of our high-technology culture—to be able to take control and unplug the telephone. Do you have the nerve?

In any case, you need to have some isolation from interruptions in order to concentrate on your writing. We've looked at some of the more extreme techniques for achieving this isolation, and you will no doubt think of others yourself. So do it any way you can, but above all, *do it.* Get yourself and your materials off into an environment in which you can be comfortable and really enjoy the writing without interruption. You'll be amazed at the quantity and quality of writing you can achieve this way. Now let's conclude this topic by considering the best way to be isolated from interruptions: by writing at home.

Personally, I write a lot at home. I'm fortunate because my line of work allows me to do it this way. However, some of my clients require more of my time in their facilities than others, and when I first started consulting I did most of my work at my clients' facilities. However, the fact of the matter is that when I work at home my clients get better products more efficiently. This may be an option for you as well.

More and more of us are working at home these days, and your home is probably the best place for you to write. It's where you live, so it ought to be comfortable and relaxing, and you can control the interruptions much easier. In fact, I would go so far as to say my home is interruption-free. I have a wife, a son, a dachshund, and two cats. These are not interrupters, or at least I don't consider them as such. These are the reasons I work: to provide my family the home and life they enjoy. So when my wife, Susan, asks me to help with something, or Sox (one of the cats) hops onto my desk wanting to have her back scratched, or my son, Alan, asks me to fix a toy, it's fine. These little interruptions do not break my concentration because I enjoy doing these things. Once done, I return to my writing with a feeling of satisfaction and renewed energy, knowing I have provided, in some small way, something my family or pets needed.

Now everyone may not be quite so tolerant of family interruptions as I am. You see, interruptions are things that distract you from your work. My house is full of stimulants—things that inspire me to work even better. But the main point is not what these particular events actually are, but how we perceive them. Basically, we have complete control over how we will react to any event. So we get to decide whether or not we will consider some event an interruption. When we are in a comfortable environment and feeling at peace with the world, fewer of these events will seem like interruptions. *We get to decide.* Think about it.

ZERO-TIME PREPARATION TECHNIQUES:
THEY GET WHAT THEY PAY FOR!

This is the part of the chapter where I usually get into some methods for circumventing the problems that arise from the demands of an unrealistically hurried schedule. As you have no doubt noted, my philosophy is basically that if the folks we write for are unreasonable, they get what they deserve. Part of our job as competent, creative writers, is to let them know this ahead of time, so that they may (if they have the ability or inclination) set their expectations accordingly. From the previous chapters, you may have gotten the idea that I have some objection to organization and scheduling, and this is not so. I am simply against *poor* organization and *unreasonable* scheduling for one simple reason: poor organization and unreasonable scheduling tend to rush creativity. Unfortunately, there seems to be a great deal of that today, much to the detriment of quality work.

The problem arises from the profit-at-any-cost syndrome, which leads to the "employees are just another commodity" attitude so prevalent today. The people in leadership positions aren't necessarily the problem; rather, they are simply caught by it. They have budget and schedule goals to meet, or they will lose their jobs, suffer reduced benefits, and so forth. So they may simply levy those same constraints on the people who work for them. However, many people will just toe the line and agree to the unrealistic constraints with no debate or response. This, too, is a mistake, because some leaders or supervisors may begin to assume that they can levy unrealistic schedules or budgets and still get the same quantity or quality of work as before. In writing, this simply is not the case, and it is our obligation to inform these people.

When I am asked by a client (and admittedly, I have more freedom here because they are clients and not employers) to write a piece, I give the client a time and cost estimate: so many hours of writing at some cost per hour. I estimate as realistically as I can, and once agreed upon, I strive very hard to deliver the piece within those constraints. If I make a mistake in my estimate, and it takes longer, I make up the difference on my own time and I do not charge the client any more. If I err on the other side, and finish it in fewer hours than I estimated, I charge the client only for the actual time I needed. This is called honorable and ethical business practice.

However, if a client decides to alter the original arrangement and wants it done in less time than I estimated, he or she simply gets less quantity or quality. The client is getting a realistic estimate and a commitment to deliver from me, and I expect the client to modify his or her needs if he or she cannot, or will not, provide the time and budget I need. This is called getting what you pay for.

As an employed technical writer, you may not have as much flexibility, but you can use the same approach. Estimate realistically and honor your commitments, but advise the folks you work for of the consequences of tightened schedules or budgets. Then proceed to accomplish the writing according to the terms you have established.

At this point, what do you do if you are still saddled with a ridiculously short schedule, which someone, in his or her divine wisdom, has agreed to in full understanding that he or she will receive less quality or quantity? First of all, you are still ready to write the piece, just as with a reasonable schedule. I talked about the planning and attitude issues in these situations in Chapters 1 and 2, and pointed out that we would still take the time to plan and that we don't have to care very much about what we produce in these instances. These are powerful tools for fast writing: planning and not caring about the product.

Then, in writing the piece, we still need the same two assets we discussed earlier—simplicity and isolation—and another, trickery. Our simple tools and isolated environment pay dividends here, because in a rush job we will be even less tolerant of complication-induced delays and interruptions than we would under normal circumstances. We can write fast and efficiently with these assets, and speed and efficiency are of the essence. There are also a few tricks we can use to speed up our process, based on the fact that we can produce a piece with reduced quality or quantity. Let's look at these issues—quality and quantity—individually.

In terms of quantity, the scripting technique, which I described in Chapter 1, is our ally here. We do the script as usual, but we elaborate our points very tersely in the first script, and then add details incrementally as we iterate through several more scripts. We make sure we complete an entire iteration before moving to the next one, and also make sure we can always complete the next iteration in the allotted time before starting it. If possible, we let whoever we are writing the script for review the iterations as they are completed, so they can see what is coming together and let it influence the next iteration. This review process is often beneficial because the reviewers may actually reconsider their constraints as they see what they are getting. What we are doing is basically adding as much elaboration as we can in the allotted time, and ensuring that we are not out of balance, not elaborating some points in excruciating detail while neglecting others. If necessary, we can alter this balance intentionally, for example, if certain points are considered more important than others. In this manner, we produce a complete piece, elaborated to the level possible within the constraints, and either balanced or prioritized according to the wishes of those for whom we are writing.

The final piece will have less elaboration, and hence probably less clarity, than if we were permitted to complete it properly, but it will be done, to the extent possible, within the allotted time and budget. After all, this is what those we are writing for wanted, and we told them what to expect. It is a production-style, low-quality, variable-quantity technique for meeting a schedule and budget. If they consider it less than what they need, fine. Let them add extra time and increase the budget, and we will elaborate it further, bringing it as close to the necessary level of detail as the schedule or budget will permit. If they add enough time or increase the budget, they will get the level of detail they need. However, to get the piece to the proper level of detail in this manner will be more expensive than doing it right in the first place, due to the costs of the multiple iterations. *They get what they pay for, and if they had asked for what they needed in the first place, they would have paid less for it!*

In terms of quality, to produce something quickly, we can apply a technique that has come into vogue recently due to the ability to electronically save and reuse text from previous writings. Some call it effective reuse; I call it plagiarism or selfplagiarism, simply depending on whether it is someone else's or my previous writing. It's efficient, it's effective, it's boring, and it's cheap—in many ways. Many organizations love it. I don't believe in it because, to me, plagiarism is plagiarism. I am not going to write a piece for a client and then plagiarize it and sell it to another client for about the same price; this is unethical and dishonorable. If I sell it at lesser cost to the second client, he or she is basically being subsidized by the first client. Either way, it is a distasteful practice, in my opinion. Furthermore, there are legal and copyright issues as well, which are not to be trifled with.

However, this is certainly not the only distasteful practice to be found in our culture, and some organizations consider anything they produce a resource for reuse, regardless of how it originally came into being. So if you are forced to use this technique, here is a pointer on how to do it quickly and forget about it. Basically, you simply modify the subject and conclusion sentences (usually the first and last ones) of the paragraphs to suit your particular needs. You fit things into your script and modify your elaboration to "glue them in." This really goes a long way in a short time. In fact, you can actually change the apparent voice, tense, and person of a piece by only making these changes to the subject and conclusion sentences, and you can actually get away with it. It's not good usage or grammar, but it's fast and it works. I considered giving an example here, but this would be akin to providing an example of how to construct a bomb. Some things are better left unsaid. The result will be a fairly acceptable (to all but those who appreciate proper usage and grammar), low-quality piece that can be constructed rapidly from other writings.

So now we've come to the end of Chapter 3, as well as to the conclusion of the first part of our little book, on the written document. In this chapter, we've looked at the essentials of actually doing the writing—simplicity and isolation—and also at some techniques and trickery for getting something written fast. I hope this will be useful to you. In this part of the book, we've also covered the essence of preparing a document, in the context of our three essential attributes: planning, attitude, and execution. Next, we'll look at how we can apply these same attributes, as well as some of the particulars we've used in writing, to preparing and making a formal presentation.

II

THE FORMAL PRESENTATION— DISSERTATION OR DISASTER

In my earlier discussions, in which I visited the art of communication in general and the written document in particular, I made the point that the essence of communication resides within three attributes: planning, attitude, and execution. Now we are ready to look into how these attributes apply specifically to the formal presentation or, for that matter, the informal one. Basically, what we have here is how these attributes may be applied to getting up in front of some folks and effectively making a point.

Returning to the basics, I want to emphasize that planning, attitude, and execution are highly interdependent attributes, as Figure II.1 illustrates, and that they form the foundation of any technical communication event, written or oral, formal or informal. As Figure II.1 shows, every time we plan well, it builds our confidence in executing the communication event. Then, the actual execution provides us feedback: success builds our confi-

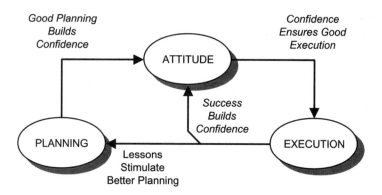

Figure II.1 The attributes and their interactions.

dence and anything else provides us a lesson for better planning or execution in future events. This entire sequence of planning, cultivating the right attitude, and executing the event actually helps us build our skills and polish our communication product, when properly done.

However, in the presentation event, this feedback is obviously more immediate and interactive than for a written document, because our audience is right in front of us. In fact, it can be downright sudden and surprising! Basically, in a presentation we get our feedback, good or bad, immediately. Not so in most published works in which there may be myriad reviews, distributions, and so forth before our audience actually gets to read it and make comments.

It is for precisely this reason—the immediacy of the feedback—that managing the attitude and execution steps are so critical in a presentation. Sure, we still need to plan well, but what do we do when the audience starts throwing tomatoes, or worse yet, falls asleep? We shall see that our specific approaches to planning, attitude, and execution must take on a slightly different tack than for a written document to accommodate these aspects of immediacy and interactivity.

This tack, then, is the subject of Part II of our little book, because I discussed the general importance of these three attributes in the context of the written document in Part I. Here, we look at the nuances and particulars of these foundational attributes as they specifically apply to the technical presentation, toward the goal of cultivating useful and effective presentation techniques. Again, we will begin with the planning aspect, because this is the stimulus for the other two. As we discovered before, good planning builds a confident attitude, which, in turn, ensures successful execution of the presentation.

4

PLANNING THE PRESENTATION

As with the written document, planning for a presentation should concentrate on our three fundamental communication principles: connection, flow, and reinforcement. The first step in planning a technical presentation is to establish a focus, to basically decide on the point of the whole thing. A common mistake is to focus on the technical matter itself. This is an easy trap to fall into because the technical matter is usually our personal focus. Hence, it is easy to assume that this must also be the focus of the presentation. Actually, the proper focus of the presentation is the audience. Why are they here? What are their interests in our subject? All too often, a presenter will simply discuss technical matter and assume that the audience will connect it to their interests. All this does is offer the crowd an opportunity to take a break while awaiting the next actually interesting presentation. As presenters, we are responsible for connecting to our audience.

MAKING THE CONNECTION

To make this connection properly, we must decide on how to relate the audience's interests, problems, or needs

51

to our subject, which is not always easy. It requires the extra effort of investigating the audience, rather than simply presenting the technology in a bland manner. For example, a presentation that describes the theory of neural networks is useful to an audience with interests in object recognition only if we start with the problem of object recognition and show how neural networks can work to solve this problem. In other words, we obey a certain precedence; we start with the audience's interests (problem, need, and so forth) and lead to the particular subject (technology, solution, application, and so forth). Hence, the good presenter who already has a neural network presentation from a previous activity will take the time to adapt this material into the context of object recognition. Under the same circumstances, the lazy presenter will use the existing presentation charts and expect to "wing it," that is, to make all the audience–technology connections on the fly, during the presentation. This presenter will succeed only if he or she can shout over the snoring coming from the audience, and even then probably won't.

Now, given that we have the right focus and are committed to connecting our presentation to the audience's interests, we need to plan the opening of the briefing. Because we need to connect to the audience anyway, the opening is exactly the place to do it, and to do it dynamically. Generally speaking, with the first one or two charts, we need to capture the audience's attention and build the bridge between their interests and our presentation material. The trick is to capture their attention while making it look effortless. Use graphics, but don't get carried away—no atomic bomb pictures or silly cartoons. Something metaphorical that connects their interests to our subject graphically is very effective. For example, for a neural network–object recognition presentation, we might design our opening chart as shown in Figure 4.1.

That should really keep the crowd on the edge of their

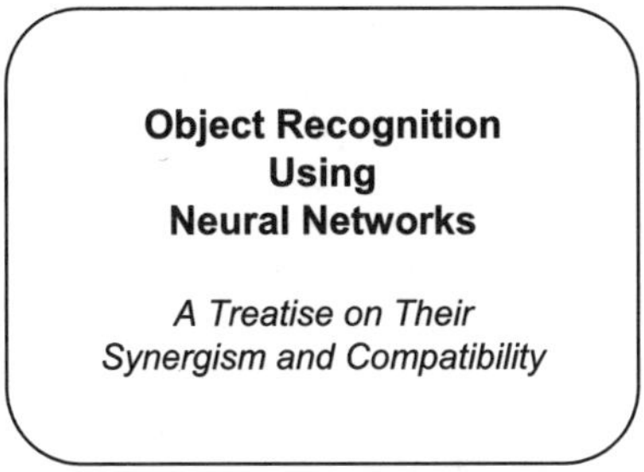

> **Object Recognition**
> **Using**
> **Neural Networks**
>
> *A Treatise on Their*
> *Synergism and Compatibility*

Figure 4.1 A stiff and boring, but otherwise appropriate opening chart.

seats—as they depart for the snack bar. It makes the connection, but is stiff, formal, and about as stimulating as a dead fish on a beach. We are generally presenting to a sophisticated audience, and we strive for dignity and sophistication in our charts, but sophistication does not imply stiffness. A logical follower to the title chart that tells the audience what particulars to expect is an agenda. A follower to the chart in Figure 4.1, given that someone is actually still in the room (and conscious), might appear as the agenda shown in Figure 4.2.

On the other hand, we can use a little creativity here and liven things up a bit. Something like the opening chart shown in Figure 4.3 will breathe some life into this

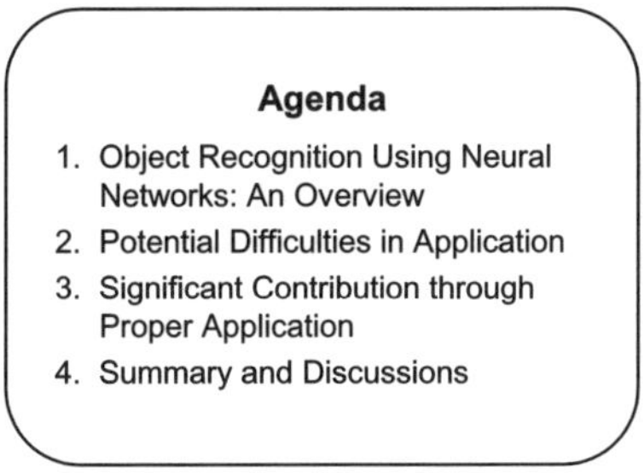

> **Agenda**
> 1. Object Recognition Using Neural Networks: An Overview
> 2. Potential Difficulties in Application
> 3. Significant Contribution through Proper Application
> 4. Summary and Discussions

Figure 4.2 A similarly stiff and boring follower to the stiff and boring opener of Figure 4.1.

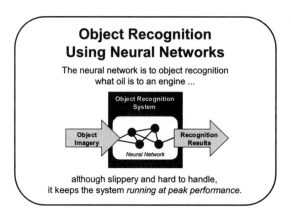

Figure 4.3 An attention-getting alternative for both opener and agenda.

cadaver. It will both make the connection and pique the audience's interest.

Let's look at what we have accomplished with this single chart. First, we made the explicit connection *from* the audience's interest (object recognition) *to* the technology (neural networks). Second, we threw in a little color (you can't see it here, but take my word for it—it's beautiful!), and graphically showed how the neural network is directly in the path of the object recognition's purpose—to extract recognition results from object imagery. Third, we indicated that neural networks may pose some difficulty (they are slippery and hard to handle). Finally, we asserted that the neural network is a significant contributor to these systems (it keeps the system running at peak performance). In other words, we have conveyed, in one interesting and eye-catching chart, the same particular information as in the two sleepers given in Figures 4.1 and 4.2, only now the audience is interested and anticipating, and not out in the lobby having potato chips and soda pop. The point is simple: we can convey the proper information effectively, maintain sophistication and dignity, and still not be boring.

PROVIDING THE FLOW AND REINFORCEMENT

Once the focus is established and we have designed our opening charts to connect the audience to our technology, we may proceed to plan the rest of the briefing. In doing so, we focus our concentration on the two remaining critical aspects: flow and reinforcement. The flow issue is that of smoothly and effortlessly taking the audience through the sequence of subjects such that the subject-to-subject transitions are seamless and comfortable. The presentation should flow like a downhill ski run, and not like a roller coaster or city street—no ups and downs, no stops and starts, just the continual, easy flow of information. This is called *building momentum and maintaining interest*. The reinforcement issue has to do with regularly returning to and providing supporting details for the central issue or issues. (The connection—remember the connection we just talked about? I hope so, otherwise I am not doing a very good job with *my* flow and reinforcement!) Because this reinforcement must necessarily diverge slightly from a particular subject, or at least represent a different level of abstraction within it, we must be careful not to upset the flow while doing the reinforcement.

Given that we take proper care of these aspects of flow and reinforcement in the course of our briefing, the audience will most likely accept whatever conclusions we present at the end, as long as these conclusions do not themselves depart from the flow and reinforcement paradigm we establish. This is only common sense. If we build our case with continual reinforcement of the central theme and appropriate validation of the particulars relevant to it, and if we bring the audience with us effortlessly and comfortably, then they should be very receptive to valid conclusions.

In general, a good way to handle these flow and reinforcement issues is to use the same tactic we used for the written document: to write a script. This script is somewhat similar to the one we looked at for the written document in Part I. It contains not merely the titles and technical content of our anticipated charts, but also the points they are to make. By planning these points, we force ourselves to attune to flow and reinforcement, because all charts in the briefing will have no other purpose. The purpose of any chart is to maintain flow and reinforcement while its content is articulating or elaborating technical aspects in support of those points. We might also develop storyboards, which permit planning both the textual and visual aspects of a briefing simultaneously. But whether or not we choose to use a storyboard, the script remains the essence of planning. For example, a script (with particular points P1, P2, and so forth) for the "Neural Networks in Object Recognition" presentation might look like this:

A SAMPLE SCRIPT

Chart 1: **Neural Networks in Object Recognition Systems** (Assume we used the one in Figure 4.3.)
- P1: Neural networks are applicable to object recognition.
- P2: To use them, problems must be overcome.
- P3: If we solve the problems, benefits are significant.

Chart 2: **A General Introduction to Neural Networks**
- P1: There is a need to understand neural networks to appreciate object recognition issues (flows from Chart 1, all points).
- P2: A basic overview will provide this understanding (flows from Chart 2, P1).

Chart 3: **Potential Difficulties to Be Overcome**
- P1: Our understanding allows us to appreciate the problems (flows from Chart 2, P2).
- P2: (Multiple charts) A discussion of specific problems in the context of object recognition is necessary (flows from Chart 3, P1, reinforces object recognition application).

Chart 4: **Contributions to More Effective Object Recognition**

P1: Our understanding of neural networks allows us to anticipate their advantages (flows from Chart 2, P2.)

P2: Our understanding of difficulties allows us to overcome (avoid) them for object recognition (flows from Chart 3, P2; reinforces object recognition theme).

Chart 5: Summary

P1: Neural networks are effective enhancements to object recognition systems, because (a) benefits are great (flows from Chart 4, P1); and (b) difficulties can be overcome (flows from Chart 4, P2).

P2: Neural neworks are valuable in object recognition (flows from Chart 5, P1a and P1b; reinforces object recognition theme and validates initial assertions from Chart 2).

Now let's look at how well we have attended to flow and reinforcement in this script. We started with a central topic (object recognition) and initially asserted that neural networks are applicable, but we must overcome problems to apply them successfully. We next provided sufficient background so that the audience could appreciate our discussions. Then, we proceeded to discuss the problems, benefits, and ways to mitigate the problems. Finally, we concluded that our initial assertions were valid and that neural networks may indeed be applied successfully and beneficially to object recognition. Hence, we *flowed* from the audience's interest, to a technology, to how that technology may be applied (and its problems mitigated), to logical and valid conclusions. We also continually *reinforced* the central theme of object recognition in all our scripted charts. Makes you want to run right out and buy a neural network and stuff it into an object recognition system, doesn't it? And guess what—we haven't actually designed a single chart or inserted the first technical detail yet!

This brings up another interesting point, which was also made in Part I, regarding the written document. We can actually plan an effective briefing, in the audience's context, without knowing a thing about the technology itself. Obviously, insertion of the technical details is essential to creating the presentation, but not to the scripting. Furthermore, in scripting first and inserting technology second, we will always avoid an out-of-context presentation.

Notice also that we did not write elaborated introductions and summaries into our presentation script as we did for the written document script, back in Chapter 1. These are not necessary for the presentation script, because we are striving to make succinct, concise points in our charts, and will verbally expand on them during the presentation. We might make some accompanying notes to assist us, if we choose. These notes could be a more fully elaborated script, basically detailed to whatever level we require to prompt ourselves to present the charts correctly. The level of detail varies among individuals. Some presenters like to use elaborated notes and others prefer simply to talk from the charts. It's a matter of style and experience. However, we never, never make elaborate, lengthy, textual charts and simply read them to the audience. The United Nations has rules strictly forbidding torture of this kind.

Given that we have created a good script, and now are going to populate it with some marvelous technology, there are additional considerations. I offer these as a few useful hints and a structural concept. First, here are the hints:

1. *Design the charts to implement the flow.* Graphical techniques can work effectively toward the total presentation flow and reinforcement of the central theme. We needn't go into the details here, but you should be aware of the graphical opportunities and take advantage of them. Graphics or cognitive science professionals can help us with this aspect, which will at least include:

- Mixing symbols or icons for interest—the same ones repeated over and over again become boring, but wide divergence can detract from the flow. Find a happy medium.
- Repeating subparts of an earlier graphic to set the context for subdiscussions of an earlier, general discussion—the "exploding" diagram.
- Properly using shape, color, texture, and position.

2. *Correlate the visual and verbal parts of the presentation.* In other words, we should think about what we are going to be saying as we design the presentation. Here, we must also consider the timing of the charts and how long a given chart will be viewed. If a chart is complex, but we are planning only a few comments, it will depart before the audience is ready for it to leave. Conversely, a long-winded dissertation formed about a simple chart will have the opposite effect: cause the audience to depart (at least mentally, if not physically) before we are ready for them to leave.

3. *Have transitions and conclusions.* This may seem obvious, but I have seen countless presentations that, in part or in their entirety, flow nicely through a sequence of points, and then abruptly end. Then the presenter and audience just stare at each other like frogs in a pond, wondering what to do next. We need to close major subparts as well as the briefing itself with a few summary remarks or conclusions, and use these to transition to the next subpart or to make the intermediate or final connection to, or reinforcement of, the central theme. We keep the flow going and we constantly reinforce. Our script should enforce this.

Now for the structural concept. It is very easy to apply the scripting technique and the hints just discussed and to achieve the connection, flow, and reinforcement we desire. What we require to accomplish this is a sound appreciation of what comprises a briefing: its elements. So let's look at the elements of a briefing.

In my mind (which admittedly wanders around a lot and needs something to keep it focused), there are only two different elements of a briefing. Once again, by keeping to a simple concept and a small set of things to deal with, we can stay focused and organized. The elements of a briefing are the categoric types of charts we can produce, and there are only two: the object chart and the text chart, as illustrated in Figure 4.4.

An object chart focuses on its object. That's obvious, isn't it? It has a central picture, drawing, or photograph—basically something nontextual—which is the point of the chart. Now just because we call it an *object chart* does not mean that it is totally devoid of text. However, the text has a supporting role: to enhance, clarify, or supplement the information on the object itself. Such textual supple-

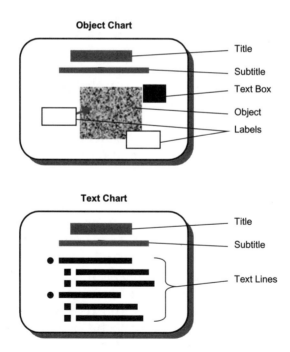

Figure 4.4 The two types of charts—object and text.

ments may be text boxes or labels associated with certain areas of the object, perhaps through overlay or pointer (arrow) techniques, as the object chart in Figure 4.4 depicts. There may also be a hierarchy to the object itself, perhaps as exploded details of certain portions of the object for example. However, for our purpose here, let's keep it simple and consider the object chart to consist of the object and the textual supplements, which is all we need to discuss connection, flow, and reinforcement in the briefing. The object chart also has a title, and perhaps a subtitle, to set its theme (what it is) and its context (how it relates to other topics in the briefing).

The text chart, also shown in Figure 4.4, is typically a sequence of statements in some sort of hierarchy. Points are made succinctly and clearly, with each subordinate point in the hierarchy somehow embellishing upon the information given in the level above it. We may, once again, mix types and add some graphical objects within the text chart, but these can be considered supplemental objects to the textual points. Such objects need to be small, with coarse detail, and not too numerous. If we create a text chart whose objects compete with or overshadow the text, then it is really not a text chart but an object chart, and we treat it that way. As with the object chart, the text chart typically has a title and perhaps a subtitle.

Given, then, that we have only two kinds of charts to deal with, the next aspect is how we go about achieving the connection, flow, and reinforcement we desire. Our script has set the general framework for achieving these attributes, but now we need to implement them within the charts themselves. Although there is no absolute method for every occasion, Figure 4.5 shows how we can generally achieve this goal. Next, we will look at how connection, reinforcement, and flow can be realized in the charts, in that order. I discuss connection and reinforcement first, because there are variations of flow based on the briefing structure, which are best explained after the other two attributes.

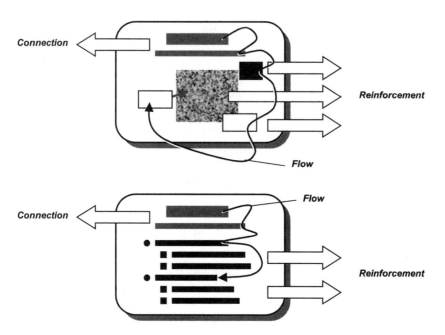

Figure 4.5 Connection, flow, and reinforcement in the two chart types.

First, let's look at the *connection*. We try, to the extent possible, to maintain some part of the connection in the titles or subtitles. We never want the audience to forget why they are receiving the briefing. So, for example, if we have a chart on how a low-pass filter improves the efficiency of a neural network in an object recognition, we might use the following title and subtitle combination:

THE LOW-PASS FILTER (Title)
BETTER NEURAL-NETWORK EFFICIENCY FOR OBJECT RECOGNITION (Subtitle)

Had we used only the title, the audience would only know that the chart is about a low-pass filter. The first part of the subtitle (Better Neural-Network Efficiency) connects the filter to its application: the neural network. Then the second part (for Object Recognition) reminds the audience that the purpose of talking about neural networks is to show how they solve the problem of object recognition, which is the audience's interest. So we have made a complete connection from the specific issue of the chart, all the way to the audience's interest, just by using a few extra words in the subtitle. Believe me, it's worth the few extra words. If the briefing is very hierarchical, it becomes more difficult to make the complete connection at the lower levels of the hierarchy, because it simply requires so many words that the title and subtitle become too long and clumsy. The guidelines are (1) to avoid complicated, multilevel hierarchical briefings in the first place, and (2) not to try to force the complete connection into every chart's title or subtitle, just where it works. Actually, the psychologists tell us that intermittent reinforcement is more effective anyway. Use your common sense and intuition, and think in the audience's context. Are they getting lost? Will they see the connection easily? Just make sure the audience gets the connection often enough to appreciate how the topics fit into their needs and interests.

Now, we can consider the *reinforcement*. Reinforcement is simply the objects and text themselves. They need to contain the essential information to make the point of the chart. For example, for our chart on how low-pass filtering makes neural networks more efficient (for object recognition), a good object chart might have some graphical results of measuring an efficiency metric, before and after the filter is added. A textual chart might have numerical results of that testing. Just remember that the reinforcement should be quantified, convincing, and substantive. This is not the place to simply regurgitate the title and promises; rather, this is the place to deliver the goods.

Finally, we can consider *flow*. There are two issues. The first is intrachart flow (on the individual charts themselves), and the second is interchart flow (from chart to chart in the briefing framework). There are also variations on interchart flow. We will begin with the intrachart case.

Intrachart flow was depicted in Figure 4.5 as the arrowed line meandering among the various elements of the charts, on the two chart types. For the text chart, it's easy. Just follow the hierarchy that makes sense. For the object chart, flow can be tricky and needs to be considered carefully. Given the natural flow from title to subtitle, the next things we want to cover when briefing the chart are the important aspects of the object. Ideally, we would like to move around the circumference of the object, going from label to label, with an occasional excursion to a text box. Although psychologists will tell us that the clockwise direction is preferred, I am not convinced that this actually matters. The central idea is to move along sequentially so the audience stays with us. If we start bouncing back and forth among the labels and text boxes like a ping-pong ball, most audiences will find something more interesting to think about. Don't make the chart a puzzle for the audience to solve—make it a comfortable flow and an easy journey. If you want a summary of the chart, just use a text box and locate it toward the bottom of the chart. Then, once the topics are covered, a transition to the final text box is not at all disruptive.

Interchart flow is largely a function of how the whole briefing is organized, and we do not have the space to cover all possible aspects of this in our little book. However, we can easily get the idea from a couple of examples. First, let's look at Figure 4.6, which shows a sequential series of a text chart, an object chart, and another text chart. The main idea is to make sure that the last thing we talk about on one chart leads into the next. In this example, the last point on the first text chart is being elaborated on the object chart Therefore, we want that last point on the first text chart not only to make its point, but also lead into the object chart. Similarly, the last label on the object chart is being explained by the second text chart. In this instance, we want that final label on the object chart to lead into the final text chart. These transitions can often be done easily by using a few extra words such as *to be explained next,* or *(next chart).*

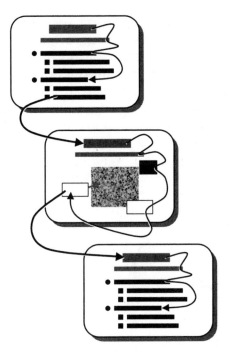

Figure 4.6 Flow in a sequence of charts.

If many words are needed to make the transition, an extra line or text box may be added. The bottom line is never to leave a chart without saying where we are going next. This is disruptive to the flow.

"But what about modularity and reuse of existing charts?" you might ask. Yes, I know we all want to create things and use them over and over again, but these are only a few transition lines, folks. If you must, save your charts in generic form and just put reminders in where the transitions are to be placed. Then when you are creating the briefing from old material, add the appropriate transitions. Please do not reuse something to death—it gets stale and it shows. Not only will the material be stale, but your enthusiasm for briefing it will be as well.

As a final example of interchart flow, let's look at a

case in which we depart from the normal flow for elaboration. Figure 4.7 shows a text chart and two object charts we want to use to elaborate on one of the text chart's points. Flowwise, we depart from the point of interest on the text chart, and then elaborate that point in the sequence of two object charts. But now we have apparently ventured down a path with no return, having left the text chart's flow before we finished it. The solution is to place a repeat of the text chart in the overall sequence right after the two object charts. This permits us to get back into the main flow without losing the audience.

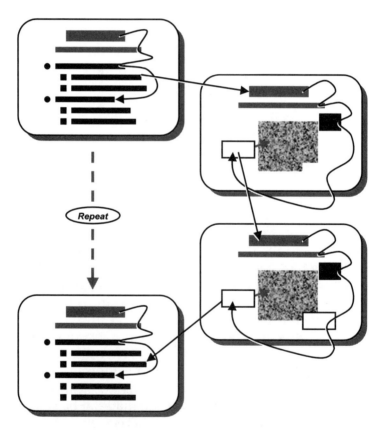

Figure 4.7 Departing from the main flow for elaboration.

There are many possible variations on interchart flow, and we haven't the space here to cover all of them. Besides, it's not necessary to cover them all. The basic principle is a simple one: always keep the flow going, even if you have to repeat an earlier chart to regain the context. Remember that it is up to us, when we plan and present a briefing, to keep the audience with us. Flow is the mechanism that allows us to do this, and it is always worth a few extra repeater charts to achieve this goal.

In summarizing the planning aspect, I want to underscore that the key issues are audience *connection, flow,* and *reinforcement.* A good presentation plan, devised with these issues in mind and supported by a good script, effective graphics, and proper verbal–visual correlation, will result in a well-prepared presentation.

ZERO-TIME PLANNING

"Good grief, here comes more bashing of poor organizers and thoughtless planners," you say. Well, surprise! I'm not going to do that here. Basically, the attitudes and motives that force the last-minute planning of a briefing are the same as those that force the last-minute planning of a document, which we talked about sufficiently in Chapter 1. The fundamental solution is the same as well: let whoever asked for the product on an unrealistic schedule know what to expect. A little verse just popped into my head as I was writing this. It makes the point perfectly:

If you plan it fast,
It will not last!

This little verse (appropriate for a little book, by the way) simply says that if you hurry the planning, or skip it altogether, your presentation will not leave a lasting impression on the audience. So do the planning as best as you can in the allotted time, and send a copy of the verse to the folks who need it most.

Whatever you do, don't combine a bunch of charts from two or three other presentations, with different forms and formats, hang a title on them, and go with it. These types of presentations not only kill any hope of having a flow, but are actually an insult to the audience— and they will respond accordingly (tomato-slinging time). I have seen countless presenters stand up and start their hurriedly put together presentation by saying, "I apologize for the shape this is in. It's an accumulation from some other presentations." Translation: "I didn't care enough about you folks in the audience to go to any trouble." What a way to start!

Something we can do, though, as we construct our presentations and start to accumulate a library of them, is to keep the reinforcement and flow separate. Say, for example, we have a scripted set of charts with all the flow points made and are ready to insert the technical details. We stop here and save the charts as they are, with their flow-oriented titles and points. This part of the briefing is peculiar to the particular event. Now, we make our reinforcement points (the technical matter) on blank forms, so they may be inserted into the flow-oriented charts for a complete package, and save them separately. Finally, we index the technical points by technical subject so we can find them again.

Look at what we have done. We have a library of technical matter that is not event specific. Now, if we have to hurriedly gather this material into a briefing, we have no conflicting form or format. If time permits, we plan and integrate these existing topics into a flow sequence that we create simply and rapidly. If not, we make title and conclusion (summary) charts and go with the topic charts as they are. If we consistently title our topics at the bottom and our flow at the top of the charts, we will automatically have topic titles as well, and can possibly make the flow work verbally. Basically, this lets us reuse other presentations without insulting the audience, which is about all we can hope for if we are forced to rush.

One more thing before we move on to the presentation attitude issues. If you make your own charts, get smart, get simple, and get rid of the fancy graphics package or illustration software you are using. Don't try to work in some complicated application that gives you more flexibility than you need and makes gigabyte-length files. Use something that works fast, makes small files, and has no more graphics capabilities than are necessary. Microsoft's Powerpoint is a decent tool but still, in my opinion, is overly complicated. As with the word processor, Word, the best thing to do is to go to the formatting and options menus and disable all the automatic functions. Then you have something close to useful. My preferred chart-making tool, a simple graphics application called SmartDraw, cost about $50. I didn't like paying $34 more for the chart maker than I paid for the word processor, but it works fine. Now, on to Chapter 5, a personal favorite of mine, where we will discuss proper attitude.

5

ACQUIRING THE SUCCESSFUL PRESENTATION ATTITUDE

I introduced the issue of proper attitude earlier, in Chapter 2, in the context of the written document. You may recall (or maybe not, if you thought Chapter 2 was boring) that I said that developing a good writing attitude is based on three things: preparation, anticipation, and enthusiasm. Developing a good presentation attitude has to do with three things as well, but only one is the same as for the written document. The first is *preparation,* and that's the same as before. The second is *precaution,* which is not quite the same as anticipation, which implies confident expectation; this has more to do with prudent fore-thought or wariness. The third is *indifference,* which is quite the opposite of enthusiasm.

So now you probably think I am a lunatic. Maybe I am. After all, I am a technologist who enjoys writing (or maybe a writer who enjoys technology). Am I contradicting myself? In Chapter 2, I talked about anticipating doing a good job for our readers and becoming enthusiastic about pleasing them. Now, here I am, a scant three chapters later, talking about exercising precautions and being indifferent to the audience. Why do we care about readers and distance ourselves from an audience? The simple answer is that because readers, as a class, care about us and an audience may not. We simply respond in kind.

Let's look at this aspect a little closer before we get into this chapter's material in earnest. Readers of a technical paper, report, article, or book will generally begin reading the document because they want to. There is some aspect of the work that interests them, for whatever reason. Then, if the document loses their interest, for the most part they simply put it aside. Some may write a critical letter to the periodical in which the work appears, and some may return the book. But basically, if readers do not like the material, they simply stop reading.

An audience is another matter altogether. It will certainly include individuals genuinely interested in the topic. However, it will most likely also include many individuals whose purpose is not to gain an appreciation of the subject matter at all. There will be those already predisposed against the topic who may want to debate it. There will be some who are in attendance against their wishes (basically, their bosses ordered them to attend). These folks may become impatient because they simply want to get it over with. Also, there will be some individuals with competing ideas who may try to deride the presentation topic to further their own goals. So, in addition to an interested segment of the audience, we have protagonists, hurriers, and debaters to contend with. Furthermore, these folks have the ability, within the constraints of the forum and good manners (don't count on this one), to disrupt the whole thing.

Now you can see the difference between readers and an audience. Readers will respond mostly to the quality of the product—the document—and not in a manner that can disrupt the activity. Has a reader ever called you on the telephone and told you to change part of a document before it was published? Not likely, unless they are clairvoyant (and even less likely if you disconnect your telephone as I suggested in Chapter 3). So we can anticipate the readers' needs and be enthusiastic about pleasing them. They can't bother us until after we finish the work. An audience, on the other hand, has so many different agendas that they are nearly impossible to please as a whole, and they can hassle us while the presentation is in progress. So our best attitude is to be outwardly confident and cooperative, yet somewhat indifferent.

This attitude is vital to the success of our presentation. We must be confident, assertive, and authoritative about our subject matter, humble and cooperative with the audience, yet indifferent to their reactions to our presentation. So what *is* the proper attitude? Simply, it is that we will succeed because failure is not one of the possible outcomes of a technical presentation. What, then, are the possible outcomes of a technical presentation? It's really quite simple: understanding and acceptance. The audience, as a whole, either understands or does not understand our presentation, with each individual being at some point between these extremes. Similarly, they either accept, or believe, our presentation or they do not, again to varying individual degrees. And that is really all there is to it. However, some presenters add extra baggage to the event: they seek fulfillment from their audience. This is not only unnecessary but foolish, as illustrated in Figure 5.1.

My point here is simply that we can go into a presentation expecting a satisfactory outcome because we are well prepared, having done the planning discussed in Chapter 4, and because there are no unsatisfactory outcomes.

Consider the possibilities. If the audience both understands and accepts our presentation, we have created a pretty good one, and we can plan to use these techniques again. If they understand it but do not accept it, we need

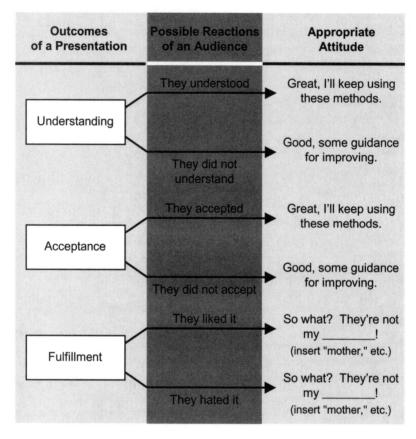

Figure 5.1 Outcomes, reactions and attitudes.

to work on our presentation paradigm (flow and reinforcement), because somewhere we lost the audience. We did not use our reinforcement properly to support our flow to a conclusion. If they accept it but do not understand it, then we need to work on technical support and presentation within the charts. We actually did the flow so well that the reinforcement, although inadequate, didn't matter. (Yes, this actually happens. I once had someone approach me after a presentation and say, "I agree with you 100 percent on that topic. By the way, I really did not un-

74

derstand the theoretical basis you presented.") If this happens to us frequently, we might consider a career change to a more sales-oriented field (such as consumer product marketing), in which gaining someone's acceptance without their understanding the product is of the essence. If the audience both did not understand and did not accept, we need to work on everything—flow, reinforcement, and technology presentation.

Finally, we should not try to realize personal fulfillment from presentations, unless we are going to become professional presenters (talk show hosts, carnival barkers, etc.). Also, we should never let an audience's reaction affect our self-esteem. (Who cares about these people's likes and dislikes anyway?) We are simply there to present and discuss a particular technology, not to win their eternal gratitude.

The essence of our attitude, then, is simply to maintain a healthy one. We plan and prepare well, expect to present successfully, and look upon any problems within the event simply as stepping-stones to become even better at presenting. We do not seek personal fulfillment and we do not accept the notion of failure, because it does not enter the picture at all. Now let's look at how the preparation process can enhance our attitude.

PREPARING TO PRESENT

Preparing for the presentation deals with both physical and mental preparation, as discussed in Chapter 3 for the written document. The physical preparation is easy and I shall not dwell on it here. Assuming we did our planning, wrote our scripts, and designed our charts well, we should simply go about creating the charts with whatever support we have available to us.

Basically, just get the charts done with ample time to review them before the actual event. By the way, if you do your own charts, seriously consider SmartDraw, the $50 graphics application we talked about earlier. With a fancy and elaborate chart maker, you will spend most of your time fussing with all the options you have instead of creating succinct, powerful charts.

Preparing mentally for the presentation is simple. We know we have planned well, we have the charts in front of us, and we have a set of notes. With all this in hand, our attitude is one of confidence. We have all the ammunition we need for this presentation, and all we have to do is step up to the line and start firing. But maybe, just maybe, we should take time for a little target practice first. Can we fire our presentation smoothly and fluently? Or will it be more like operating a rusty flintlock? Can we cover the material in the allotted time? Or will we still have most of our rounds in the clip after the target has gone by? We had better find out.

To rehearse or not to rehearse? That is the question. I don't think a full-blown rehearsal in front of a mock audience of colleagues is very useful. These people will not have the same agendas as those in a real audience, and it is really difficult to behave in front of your colleagues as you would in front of an actual audience. You might as well rehearse in front of a cat. The best way to practice is simply to get comfortable and look through your charts, think through your words as you go, and time yourself. After a few sorties of this nature, you'll have it down pat. However, this activity will sometimes precipitate chart changes. If you start the whole process early enough, you'll have plenty of time to change the charts. Getting through these previews will also build your confidence, which is the key to a good attitude, and the true value of any rehearsing.

TAKING THE PROPER PRECAUTIONS

Having planned the presentation, created it according to the script, reviewed it, modified it as necessary, and reviewed it again a few times, we may think we are ready to give the presentation. If we could be isolated from the audience in a nice, soundproof, glass room, that would be true. But that is not typically the case, unless you happen to be the dictator of an unstable, coup-inclined republic! For most of us, taking precautions means anticipating the agendas of the diverse audience we will encounter and deciding how to deal with them.

The way we do this is by taking a few more excursions through the presentation charts, this time in the context of the audience. What will a reluctant participant think about the length? How will a nitpicker react to a particular technical point? What fault will an advocate of a competing technology find with certain principles? These are the questions we ask ourselves as we go through the charts in this manner. Then, we decide what we will do about it. Maybe we will have a few backup charts or other material to counter an argument. Or maybe we will have tomatoes of our own to throw back at them. By conducting this type of review and preparation, we continue to build our confidence. We were already prepared for the expected, and now we are ready for anything, or almost anything.

DEVELOPING A HEALTHY INDIFFERENCE

Developing a healthy indifference is sealing our attitude in an impregnable coat of armor. We have planned, created, improved, reviewed, and taken the proper precautions. We have done all we can possibly do, so what is left? Nothing, that's what! So, accordingly, because we have nothing left to worry about, we might as well start thinking about whatever comes after the presentation. We move on to our next agenda.

Basically, we take the attitude that we have prepared as well as we can and that we really don't care enough about the audience's likes and dislikes to concern ourselves any further. We'll handle anything that comes up when it does, and that is that. We certainly aren't going to spend every waking moment between now and the time of the presentation redoing our already complete preparation. That would be silly. We definitely aren't going to sit around scrutinizing our notes just prior to the event. We've seen them enough already. Our attitude is that we are already past the event, and it has no more significance than going to the grocery. We don't get worked up about a trip down the frozen-foods aisle, and we aren't going to get worked up about this presentation either.

You'll be amazed at the feeling of freedom and relief this attitude brings. You'll feel loose, confident, and ready to go. If you do it right, you'll avoid all traces of pre-event nervousness, and the whole thing will simply work out. By becoming aloof and detached in attitude, we place the significance of the event where it belongs—somewhere among the routine chores and not up with the actually significant happenings of our lives. Then, we just go and do it, and don't worry at all about how the presentation may be received by the audience.

ZERO-PLANNING ATTITUDE ADJUSTMENTS

I don't have a lot to say here, simply because our attitude doesn't change when we are asked to jump into a presentation with no planning or preparation time. A good presentation attitude is just that, and it doesn't need any adjustments just because we lack adequate time. We are always prepared because our attitude is that whatever preparation we have done is sufficient, by definition, and that the audience really doesn't matter. We also have the attitude that anyone who asks for a rush job gets what he or she deserves. So what do we do when we're asked for an "instant presentation"? How do we compensate for an unreasonable request? The answer is simple: we say "fine" and just do it.

We use what we already have, we don't worry about the audience, and we certainly don't concern ourselves over this situation. We just step up and have fun with it. Our attitude is constant: that we are prepared and in control and that the audience is simply nothing to worry about. In the next chapter, we will look at how that attitude carries us through the actual presentation.

CHAPTER

6

CONDUCTING THE PRESENTATION

I could spend pages and pages on the art of executing a presentation (but then this little book would be in danger of becoming a big book, a fate worse than being chewed up by the cat). There are volumes full of useful information, tips, and tricks to help the presenter. From these sources, we can learn how to stand, gesture, talk, move, interact with the audience, and so forth. However, the fact of the matter is that all these aspects (which appear in big books, by the way) are founded on only three basic elements, and once in command of these elements, we are ensured of success. These elements are *poise, confidence,* and *dignity.*

So how do we acquire these traits? Take a seminar? No, that would just cost a lot of money and get us another big book or two. Go back to school? No, some of those instructors were pretty boring; we can learn how to be pretty boring by ourselves. Watch some talk shows? Get serious! Emulate a great orator? No, the truly great ones are all dead, and we certainly aren't going to emulate that. Could it be that we already have these traits within us and just need to turn them loose? Yes! Let's consider them one at a time.

POISE

Poise deals with how we visually appear and present ourselves as we talk. When poised, we speak well and clearly, gesture appropriately (not excessively), and let our body language affirm our presentation. We do not appear nervous (because we aren't), and the presentation flows easily and fluently. To maintain poise, a good rule to remember is simply to s-l-o-w d-o-w-n. When we are in front of an audience, we sometimes tend to get into a rush. When this happens, our words become slurred, our gestures become frantic, and we move from topic to topic like a ping-pong ball. We can become a total mess in a matter of seconds. When we get frantic the audience gets nervous too, and then they become a total mess as well. Slow down and take your time. A poised person in front of an audience is comfortable and moves from topic to topic at a reasonable rate, taking time to explain everything properly and chatting with the audience occasionally. There is no hurry, and the audience will respond very well to a poised, unhurried, and congenial presenter. So how can we acquire such poise? That's easy—by being confident. Confidence breeds poise. It's as simple as that. Furthermore, the reason we are poised is *not* that we have learned ninety-six ways to *appear* confident. It is because we *are* confident.

CONFIDENCE

We are confident because we have planned well and prepared our presentation as a fluid, comfortable, enjoyable encounter with an audience we don't give a hoot about. Our planning has considered the audience's needs, interests, and diverse agendas, and we have taken steps to ensure that our presentation makes the *connection* to them, and proceeds with proper *flow* and *reinforcement*. But we really don't care if the whole lot of them are suddenly transported to Mars right before our very eyes. So our confidence is naturally high whenever we have done the planning and nurtured the correct attitude, as discussed in Chapters 4 and 5. With such confidence, we are ready for anything.

DIGNITY

Now that we have poise and confidence, you might ask, "But what happens when something goes wrong?" Simple. That is when we require dignity. Everyone makes mistakes and may even present erroneous information from time to time. Audiences can be forgiving of errors or problems, as long as we make an honest and dignified recovery from them. On the other hand, nothing will sink a presentation faster than the presenter falling apart after encountering a problem.

There are many kinds of mechanical problems we cannot foresee, such as projection systems failing or fire alarms going off (not to mention buttons popping off and hitting the microphone). These incidents are best handled by simply correcting them, if we can, or waiting them out while remaining calm and dignified. A prolonged interruption is a good time to sit back down and wait with the audience while the facility maintenance crew does their job to repair the offending machinery. Our job is not to entertain the audience while an interruption gets resolved, so we simply join the audience in awaiting a solution. This takes the pressure off *us* as presenters. We and the audience collectively have a problem and simply await its solution.

Other problems may be in the form of a member of the audience taking exception to a point in the briefing. This is not a problem because the interrupter might actually be correct. However, if we stop to dwell on the issue, it can disrupt our flow and cause us to lose the audience. Here, it is best to say something like, "You have a good point, but my time is limited. I would like to complete my presentation to the audience. Perhaps later we could get together to discuss your idea."

What have we done here? First, we have avoided a confrontation by conceding that this person may be correct, thus diffusing the undignified argument that might have ensued. Second, we have aligned the audience with us by implying that we and the audience collectively want to continue past the interruption. Hence, the interrupter who insists on immediate attention must do so against the audience's wishes. Finally, we have agreed to settle the issue later, so the interrupter will potentially have the opportunity to assert the point to us. It is perfectly fine to move past an interruption by deferring the discussion to a later time. This will preserve the flow of the presentation and still satisfy the interrupter. To stop and defend a point excessively when it is not part of the plan is folly. Park your ego and keep your dignity. Always align yourself with the audience and against the interruption, regardless of its source.

By the way, "regardless of its source" includes the person who is in charge of the session as well as all other interrupters. One of the rudest and most insulting experiences for a presenter is to have a disorganized person who is in charge try to make real-time adjustments to the schedule. Typically, this individual has allowed most of the earlier presenters to overrun their time allotments, and now wants the later presenters to cut back. What fun it is to see these folks sweat over their own doing.

These cases are opportunities for some good sport. If the person in charge asks you to shave time off your presentation in advance, just smile. Why settle the issue here when it can be more fun right in front of the audience? During your presentation, as you reach the time when this person wants you to stop, there will usually be some kind of signal. It might be the person himself or herself, waving frantically or going through another kind of gesturing frenzy to get your attention, or it might be a flashing light or sound. If the audience can't perceive the signal, ignore it and just continue.

But, if the esteemed session chairperson actually interrupts or otherwise catches the audience's attention, it's time for the kill. Stop what you are doing, and call the audience's attention immediately and blatantly to this person. If you can, have the house lights turned on. Then say, "I am in the midst of a presentation for which I have spent considerable time and trouble to prepare for this audience. I am within my allotted time, and I need the rest of it to finish properly. Do you want me to stop now without finishing what I have started?" If you get a "no," which is most often the case, get back into your flow and finish. If you get a "yes," just walk off the stage and let this person recover, if he or she can. These people cause their own problems and it's not up to us to compensate for them.

Let me tell you about one of my personal experiences. I was attending a seminar, and in the midst of one of the presentations, the chairman started tinkling a little bell. I guess he thought it would be a subtle way to remind presenters that it was time to wind up their talks. However, the subtlety departed when the speaker suddenly clutched the podium for dear life and looked frantically around the auditorium. Then this speaker "regained his composure" and said to the audience, "I'm sorry. When I heard that tinkling sound I thought that perhaps Tinkerbell was sprinkling pixie dust on us and we were all about to float away." The audience roared, the fool stopped the tinkling, and the speaker finished his talk. This speaker was obviously experienced in dealing with interruptions. If you employ such tactics, however, you may not receive the little gift with the host organization's logo on it, or some other memento of the occasion. So what? We all have lots of trinkets like that. Personally, I give them to my son. He puts them in his tree house.

So we see that we already have poise, confidence, and dignity, and just need to use them. We also see that problems will occur and that we will simply handle them as they happen. From a simple projector bulb failure to arousing the ire of the chairperson, all problems are the same. They are just things we need to deal with as they occur. If the audience mattered, or the chairperson was important, we might get nervous. However, this is most often not the case.

ZERO-PREPARATION PRESENTING

Believe it or not, zero-preparation presenting is the most fun we can have as presenters. Why? Because what responsibility we have to an audience under normal circumstances (and that is precious little anyway) disappears altogether in this situation.

As usual, we generally find ourselves in this situation because someone has probably decided we need to drop everything and do a presentation with little or no notice. We have no preparation time whatsoever, not even to do the meager preparation I talked about in Chapter 4. Now we have to get up and talk. Are we nervous? Are we worried? Of course not! We are going to do just two things when we get up there. The first is to lay the responsibility for what is about to happen squarely on the shoulders of the genius who requested it. Having done this, the second is to do whatever we like with the presentation—just have fun with it.

It really is fun, honestly. First you say something like, "Our marketing VP asked me to drop everything and come talk to you, so here I am. If I can't explain something adequately along the way, we'll follow up later." Now you're free. Just go through whatever charts you have available, and align yourself with the audience—as a curious participant, not an authority. Here, the only difference between the presenter and the audience is that the presenter is doing most of the talking. So just say what you think the audience is thinking. Say things like, "Boy, that's a silly looking chart," and "I can't figure this one out, can you?" Just be casual and informal. You can do this and still maintain your dignity, by becoming the aloof narrator rather than the nervous presenter. You're not responsible or at fault. You're just reporting the material as you see it. Don't compensate for others' lack of planning, or you'll be doing it eternally.

Of course, this situation also applies when we are confronted with presenting something with which we have had no prior interaction, such as a presentation someone else has produced. On the other hand, we may sometimes be confronted with presenting our own material with no time for preparation. This is a little easier because we understand the material even though we haven't had an opportunity to tailor it to the audience's needs. Hence, we will have a problem with connection and possibly flow. Our existing charts may have all the reinforcement of concepts they need, but these concepts will not form a cohesive flow that is connected to the audience's interests.

The solution is simply to make the connection and accomplish the flow verbally as we present the briefing. We first need to find out about the event and the audience's interests. We may have a little time to do this, perhaps by reading promotional material for the event. In the worst case, if we have no information, we can try to arrive at the event in time to hear a keynote address or some other presenter's presentations prior to ours. We need to be creative and persistent. There is always information to be found if we look for it, and rarely do we have absolutely no time at all to determine the audience's needs. Once we know these needs, we order our existing charts as best we can to make a flow from the audience's needs to our concepts, and we plan how to verbally supplement the charts to accomplish this flow. We must rely on our cool and confident attitude, and take it slow when we deliver, so that we keep the charts and the ideas we are presenting clear and cohesive.

Here, as with the situation in which we are delivering

a presentation prepared by someone else, it is useful to be honest and open with the audience, and lay the responsibility for whatever transpires on whoever created it. A little humor mixed with the delivery and the admission to being less than perfectly prepared will produce a friendlier audience and will relax us as we present the material.

Are you worried about getting fired or reprimanded for laying responsibility where it belongs? That is not likely to happen. If you're the one tapped to handle the emergencies, you're probably too valuable to fool around with. Also, the audience will enjoy the encounter if you do it right. The presentation will be inadequate regardless, but doing it this way will keep relations with the audience in good shape. Trying to fake your way through it or going forth hesitantly and apologetically will not impress anyone.

HANDLING THE VIDEO TELECONFERENCE

Before leaving this chapter on conducting the presentation, it is worthwhile to say a few words about the impact on presentations of one of life's modernizations: the video teleconference. This is yet another attempt to complicate our lives, but certainly a manageable one. In such cases, we may be speaking to a dual audience: the one in the room with us and the one remotely connected via the teleconferencing system. The planning and attitude aspects are pretty much the same as for a live presentation. However, the mode of execution requires a slight adjustment.

Basically, we need to be aware of how we are being viewed by the remote audience. As we look at the audience in the room with us, we can both speak to them and see or hear their reactions in the same location. This is not necessarily true for a teleconference, because the monitor through which we see them and the camera by which they see us may be in different locations. So we have a bit more trouble interacting with them.

The key is to realize the locations of the camera and the monitor and treat them appropriately. It is all too easy to talk at, and look at, the monitor, but that may be pulling us away from the camera. So we may think we are talking to the remote audience but actually be facing away from them. The solution is simply to be aware of where we should be directing our gestures and where we should be facing. We make eye contact with the camera occasionally, as we do with the rest of the audience, and we glance at the monitor occasionally to get feedback on how the remote audience is reacting. It's really no trouble at all, as long as we keep our dignity and poise and do not hurry or become obsessed with talking to the camera.

Well, we've reached the end of Part II. Now we know how to plan, prepare, and execute a presentation, and most important, how to assume the right attitude. We saw that our basic attributes of connection, flow, and reinforcement pervade the planning. We noted that a healthy indifference is the key to assuming the correct attitude. We realized that poise, confidence, and dignity are the keys to a successful execution of the presentation. We looked at ways to handle zero-time situations wrought by people who may not even be sentient, much less able to organize something. We also saw that in moving from the controlled environment of document writing to the less-controlled one of presentation, we compensate by becoming less concerned about those who receive our communication. Finally, we learned how to effectively handle the video teleconference. In Part III, we are going to move from the less-controlled environment of the presentation to the chaos of the meeting.

III

THE INFORMAL DISCUSSION— *MEETINGS AND MISHAPS*

In this part of our little book (I really do like little books, you know), we are going to examine that highly interactive type of communication: the meeting. As usual, I focus on the attributes of planning, attitude, and execution, the critical issues of connection, flow, and reinforcement, and also touch on what to do if you lack the time to prepare yourself properly.

A few years ago, I worked with a gentleman who had an acronym for ineffective meetings. To him, such a meeting was a BOGSAT—bunch of guys sitting around a table. To us, BOGSATs can be avoided by first deciding which meetings are worth attending and which ones are better left alone, as I shall proceed to explain.

Similarly to the other parts of this little book, I handle the meeting in three chapters that cover planning the meeting, acquiring the right attitude for it, and then participating in it. We already have a good handle on the principles from the other two parts. We know how to plan, cultivate our attitude, prepare, and execute two types of communication events: documents and presentations. Meetings are generally a combination of the two, with a little less formalism involved in either case. However, this is not the real issue regarding meetings.

The real issue is how to select only those meetings that are effective, and then to use our principles in a situation that is very interactive and sometimes out of control. The key point regarding meetings is that most of them are useless, so more than anything else, we need to be able to identify and avoid the useless ones, as I explain in this part of our little book.

7

PLANNING FOR THE MEETING

What should we do when we are invited to a meeting? The same thing as when we are invited to sample narcotics—*just say no*. Oh-oh! Reality check here. Sometimes we have to go to a meeting. So I guess we should look at how to do it. We can approach this in the same manner as the document or presentation: through planning, attitude, and execution. The real problem, however, is how to determine which meetings we actually should attend. So first let's look at which meetings are useful and which are not.

ATTENDING OR AVOIDING MEETINGS

Meetings are different things to different people, but there are basically three types: (1) excuse meetings, (2) support meetings, and (3) effective meetings (which, by definition, makes the first two types ineffective meetings). Some folks use meetings as excuses. They are confronted with an intractable problem and they seek to spread the blame, so to speak. If they pass the problem from themselves, alone, to a team, then the team can help shoulder the blame for the inevitable failure. If they actually get on the track to solve the problem, they can take credit for having the insight to assemble a successful team. Some people use meetings as support platforms. They lack confidence in their convictions, so they want to assemble a quorum to affirm their ideas. They populate the meeting with subordinates, nonexperts, and basically anyone who will most likely agree with them. A few—a very few—folks use meetings effectively for actual problem solving or coordination. In these cases, the meetings are characteristically short, to the point, and conclude with tangible results and specific actions for the attendees.

Many years ago, as a young scientist, I was working on a project that involved a team, mostly technologists, working on individual portions of the whole system. The project engineer, supposedly responsible for coordinating the whole effort, was forever calling meetings to discuss problem areas. We had three or four meetings every week, and they involved the whole team. Even when an issue was relevant to only one or two specialists, everyone had to attend and participate.

You can imagine what transpired. Basically, we were all so caught up in the meetings that we had no time to do our work. The schedule and budget suffered, and the project engineer, upon realizing the gravity of the situation, called a meeting (naturally) to discuss the problems. Here, one of the senior engineers laid it on the line. He told the project engineer that the reason we were falling behind was that we were spending all our time in meetings. The project engineer, on hearing this, said, "You know, you may have something there. Let's all take the action to formulate ideas on how we can meet less frequently. Since this problem is critical, we should meet every day and work on it until we have a solution."

Hello!? Anybody home in there? This project engineer not only missed the point, but made the situation worse. The fellow was basically incompetent, and his only hope to do anything was to assemble a team and hope for the best. His were the ultimate *excuse meetings*.

Embedded within these excuse meetings, we also had

the opportunity to witness the *support meeting,* because one of the senior engineers (let's call him John) would only bring with him those technical staff who would agree with, and compliment, all his designs and ideas. It was hysterical. This charlatan would have one of his subordinates introduce the subject in a very complimentary fashion, such as, "John made a real breakthrough this week, and he's going to overview his concepts for us." Then John would go through his spiel while his underlings praised him on every point. He never revealed sufficient detail to allow anyone else to actually scrutinize his work, and the project engineer was too naive to realize the ride he was on. Unfortunately for John, he designed circuits that lacked the performance they needed. Then, suddenly, John converted to the excuse meeting so we could all share in his failure. Thanks, John.

Fortunately, I have also witnessed *effective meetings.* These were often production meetings because a certain production manager in our organization had an excellent approach to meetings. "I never saw a meeting where any souls were saved after the first twenty minutes," he would say. His meetings were twenty minutes long. Everyone had a specific topic to present and a specific amount of time in which to present it. He concluded the meetings with specific actions assigned for the next one. No muss, no fuss—just points, decisions, and assignments.

Obviously, some meetings are worth attending and others are not. We need to attend and participate in the effective meeting, and avoid the other two types. So let's look at how to recognize them and respond to requests to attend first, and then investigate how we can be effective in the ones we actually do attend.

FILTERING MEETINGS

There is a simple and practical filtering process we can use to detect which type of meeting to expect, and a few others we can use to avoid those that would only waste our time. We simply ask the organizer of the meeting to define our role. Just ask specifically: (1) Why do you want me to attend? and (2) What do you want me to do? When we ask these questions, and are persistent in demanding answers, the answers can be quite revealing. Next, I illustrate a few typical answers to these questions, what they really mean, and how we might respond:

QUESTION: Why do you want me to attend your meeting and how shall I plan to participate?

ANSWER: Oh, it's just a brainstorming session on Project X. We want to get our senior scientists together and get some ideas for solving a few problems. You don't need to prepare anything special, just show up and participate.

CONCLUSION: Sounds like an excuse meeting. The only brainstorm is whatever chaotic neuron firings in this person's head make him or her think we would actually attend such a fiasco.

RESPONSE: Great. I'll need to charge a few hours to your project to review what you have done, and I'll try to formulate a few specific solutions that you can use to solve some of your problems.

This kind of response will usually scare away the inviter who seeks an excuse meeting. We are going to cost this person some project funds, and if we find a solution, it will clearly be from us, but he or she will have to implement it. He or she won't be able to spread the blame or capture the credit for a solution. However, if the inviter actually wants an effective meeting, but is simply disorganized, he or she will still want our attendance, and may organize the meeting better for the rest of the crowd as well. If the inviter simply wants an excuse meeting, he or she will generally balk, and we can simply decline to attend.

QUESTION: Why do you want me to attend your meeting and how shall I plan to participate?

ANSWER: We've just made a real breakthrough in process X, and we're going to present it to a few key people. I know this is not precisely your field, but you're a respected scientist here and I would really appreciate your attending.

CONCLUSION: Grab your boots, because it's getting pretty deep here. Sounds like a support meeting. Why would someone invite nonexperts to a technical meeting except to do a snow job?

RESPONSE: Thanks for the invitation. By the way, I've been reading up on process X lately and my friend Dr. Roberts, at the local university, is considered a national expert in this field. I'll invite him along too. I bet he'll have several useful comments for you.

Again, our response is designed to qualify (if not terrorize) the inviter. If the inviter wants a legitimate technical forum, he or she will welcome the attendance of an expert. If, however, the inviter just wants to get unqualified support for a halfbaked idea, he or she will run for the hills at the thought of such scrutiny.

QUESTION: Why do you want me to attend your meeting and how shall I plan to participate?

ANSWER: I know you work regularly with process Y. We are attempting to use it in process X, which we are developing, but we are not getting the results we expect. At the meeting, our researchers will present our approach, and we would like you to critique and advise us. If you want to review our processes and preliminary results in advance, we will provide them to you.

CONCLUSION: An effective meeting. Clear reasons for attending and specific goals.

RESPONSE: I'll be there.

Do you see the tactic at hand in all these situations? Basically, in each case we agree to attend, but do so in a manner that will reveal the true intent of the inviter. If the inviter really wants an effective meeting, then we have encouraged him or her to organize or anticipate better. If not, we will probably get uninvited because we will be perceived as a threat to his or her true motivations.

Now, given that we can detect the type of meeting we are confronted with, avoid the useless ones, and attend the effective ones, we can talk about how to actually go about planning the meeting. Actually, the first two parts of this little book have provided all the ammunition we need. We basically plan properly, acquire the right attitude, and do it. If the meeting requires documentation, we follow the document practices from Part I. If we need to make a presentation, we use the presentation techniques from Part II. Only the degree of detail and formalism will vary, because we may not need documents or charts conforming to certain standards in a fairly informal meeting. However, even armed with this ammunition, there are some nuances of the meeting that bear scrutiny. Hence, I will cover the aspects of planning here, and proceed with the aspects of attitude and execution later, in Chapters 8 and 9, respectively.

PLANNING THE MEETING

In planning the meeting, we use our three fundamental principles of communication: making the *connection,* establishing the *flow,* and providing the *reinforcement.* We make sure we understand our specific role in the meeting, and prepare any handouts, documents, or presentation material, using these three principles. Even if we are only going to be talking, without the aid of documentation or charts, we follow these principles, and may even prepare a script. Although the entire event will be much less controllable than documents or presentations, we need to have a plan for making our points. Our three principles allow us to do this.

The main thing we need to understand about meetings is that the flow is difficult to manage. Obviously, if we go to a meeting and introduce a few topics, we must have a connection between those topics and some area or areas of interest, and we must provide reinforcement or substance behind those topics. So connection and reinforcement are as essential as ever, and are easy to achieve using the documentation or presentation techniques outlined in Parts I and II. However, flow is difficult to control. Even with a set agenda and a fairly dominant meeting chairperson, attendees will tend to get off on tangents. So we cannot count on being able to present or discuss a long string of topics with some preconceived flow properly relating them to one another. For example, let's assume we are statisticians who have invented some new statistical processses that enhance computer-aided design (CAD), especially for architectural work. We first outline how CAD can enhance architectural design, then talk about how statistical estimation can achieve more effective CAD, and finally discuss how our particular statistical process designs work. Our anticipated flow therefore has the following sequence:

1. How architectural design is improved by CAD
2. How statistical processes can enhance CAD
3. How our particular statistical processes work

Now that's a good and logical flow, isn't it? We start with the problem, introduce a technique to solve it, and then rationalize the technique. We flow from the need to the solution and detail the solution. But the problem is that good and logical things are usually incompatible with meetings. For example, maybe the chairperson has decided to let everyone talk about different ways to improve architectural design, then about methods to achieve the improvements, and finally about how those methods work.

Also, let's assume that this chairperson is not opposed to sidetracks and excursions into other topics, and that outside interruptions will occur. Then, the sequence of events that will really transpire at the meeting is something like this:

1. Introductions and opening remarks
2. Ways to improve architectural design
   a. Somebody else's method
   b. Anecdote about somebody's aunt's surgery
   c. Somebody else's method
   d. How architectural design is improved by CAD (*our first topic*)
   e. Interruption by the boss
   f. Chairperson tells a joke (after the boss leaves)
   g. Somebody else's method
3. Methods to achieve the enhancements
   a. Rationale for somebody else's method
   b. Interruption by the boss's boss, whose son, Junior, is the star of the local high school football team
   c. Discussion about last Friday's football game, and how Junior spent most of the time on the bench (after the boss's boss leaves)
   d. How statistical processes can enhance CAD (*our second topic*)
   e. Rationale for somebody else's method
   f. Speculation about how medical imaging will probably be used to diagnose the football player who got smashed in last Friday's football game
   g. Rationale for somebody else's method
4. How the methods work
   a. How somebody else's technique works
   b. Complaint session about local network management
   c. How somebody else's technique works
   d. How our particular statistical processes work (*our third and final topic*)
   e. Interruption by someone who claims to be a boss, yet nobody recognizes this person

    f. Speculation about a hostile takeover by the person who claimed to be a boss (after this person leaves)

    g. How somebody else's technique works

5. Meeting ends

You see the point here. If we have a flow across multiple topics, it is going to get pretty well shattered, scattered, or splattered in the actual meeting. So we simply plan for that. We plan our documents (handouts for the meeting), and any material we might show (such as charts) using the same methods discussed in Parts I and II for documents and briefings, with one major difference: we make all the charts and handouts (documents) short, easy to understand, and self-contained with strong links to our other topics. We plan our discussions accordingly. Then, despite the fact that they are addressed among many other topics and perhaps even reordered, our topics will make sense. In other words, our flow is replaced by reminders, within both our material and our planned talks, to make sure all the relationships among topics we want to achieve are intact and are executed. It's a simple matter of adding enough reminder material to get the meeting's participants back on our track (well, that train got back in here again, didn't it?). Just think about what you would need in a handout, chart, or talk to be reminded of its predecessor, despite interruptions in between, and put that in the front end of the material. It works, and your material and discussions will have a cohesiveness that others' will lack. Your topics will be remembered and so will you, which will make it more difficult for you to hide and avoid interruptions, as discussed in Chapter 3. But that's the price of fame, I guess.

ZERO-TIME PLANNING

What happens when we are snatched into a meeting without the time to plan properly? We make plans to find a better hiding place and not be quite so visible in the future! Having thus comforted ourselves, we can do a few things to make our participation in the meeting useful despite the zero-time aspects.

First, we need to define our role in the meeting, just like we discussed earlier in this chapter. We may be able to avoid the meeting altogether if it is a support meeting or an excuse meeting, and that will be that. Second, if it is going to be an effective meeting, we may not be required to participate very substantially. If we are going to be merely a spectator or have a minor role, this will reduce the problem of planning considerably. Finally, given that we have a role and we need to provide material and talk about it, we still have a means to succeed, as illustrated next.

Assuming we generally prepare our documents and charts according to the methods given in Parts I and II, we are in pretty good shape. All we need to do is plan what material to bring and how to relate the different materials to one another and to the topic or topics we are responsible for. This takes little time, and is essentially planning the flow using existing assets. Having done this, and having made a few quick notes, if time permits, we can hand-write flow-related comments on the material we will be handing out. Conversely, lacking such time, we can plan to make the flow work verbally as we participate in the meeting. In fact, having the other participants mark their own copies of our material as we go along is a good way to keep them focused. So, in essence, the way to overcome a zero-time planning situation is to spend the time we have planning around what we already have. This is the simplifier and time-saver we need in such situations.

In summary, there are effective meetings and ineffective ones. Ideally, we qualify and attend only the effective ones. Realistically, we will probably have to attend many of the ineffective ones as well. For the meetings we have to attend, whether effective or not, our documentation and presentation principles from Parts I and II apply in varying forms. The key is maintaining the flow and planning for chaos. The U.S. Marines have a saying: "We don't plan, we improvise!" Well, I think that's a catchy phrase, but not altogether true. The Marines *do* plan, but they plan for the unexpected, so when the unexpected arrives, they can cope. We do the same for a meeting, and coping has a great deal to do with attitude. Next, we look at how to acquire the proper attitude for a meeting.

8
ACQUIRING A MEETING ATTITUDE

Our attitude for a meeting is quite similar to that for the formal presentation. We need that attitude of healthy indifference we talked about in Part II. We can't control all the participants, so we had better not care very much about their responses. We follow the steps of *preparing,* and *anticipating the unexpected.* Then we go about our business and, once prepared, look forward to whatever comes after the meeting, and get ready to enjoy the meeting as it unfolds.

PREPARING

Getting ready for a meeting, just like getting ready to write a document or to present a briefing, has two aspects: physical preparation and mental preparation. These are not unfamiliar to us, because we looked at how they applied to documents and presentations in Parts I and II of our little book. However, the uncertainty of the meeting introduces additional dimensions to these aspects.

Physical preparation is pretty much the same as that for a document or a presentation. If we have used the scripting techniques in our planning stages, preparing the physical material is essentially the same as discussed earlier for documents and presentations. The real issue in physical preparation for a meeting is not the materials, but the *environment*—what will be the logistics and choreography of the meeting room, and how we can best use this to our advantage. Earlier, I commented several times about the meeting being essentially a less-controllable situation than the document or the presentation. However, the environment is often an exception to this rule. We may actually have more familiarity with the physical space than for a document or presentation because it will often be the local conference room.

The first thing to do is pay a visit to the meeting room, ask ourselves a few questions, and do some thinking. Where will the chairperson sit? Where will we and the other participants sit? Where can the interruptions, such as doors and telephones, come from? How do we want to address the participants—sitting, standing, or moving to the front of the room? How shall we distribute materials—all at once or as they are addressed? Basically, we need to determine, based on our knowledge of what is supposed to transpire, how we will physically fit into the event. If we want to be noticed and have strong issues to address, we would be better off seated close to the point of attention, which is usually the chairperson or the projection screen (if charts will be shown). If we want to disappear into the crowd, we would be better off somewhere in the middle of the rest of the folks. If we want to escape early, we need to be close to an exit, and oblique to the gazing direction of the chairperson. There is no magic rule for all of this, and we cannot describe and resolve all possible instances in a book of any size, much less in a little book. The essence is simply to prepare and anticipate how and where we want to fit in. Think of it as a play to be choreographed, with due allowance for the unexpected, as I shall discuss later in this chapter.

Mental preparation for a meeting is very similar to

that for a presentation: we care a lot about the material, less about the participants, and very little about the outcome. We want our handouts, charts, or discussions to be polished and professional, and that is why we prepare them as we would for a document or a more formal presentation. But it's just not a good idea to get all excited over the anticipated outcome of a meeting. We probably have to care a bit more about the participants than we would about the audience for a more formal presentation, because these participants may be mostly colleagues who will be interacting with us regularly. So we are at a bit of a disadvantage here because we cannot simply brush off the participants as we would most presentation audiences.

The key is not to worry about the outcomes of a meeting, and once again to look forward to the next actually enjoyable event in our lives. Now, for some people, meetings may actually be enjoyable. I have heard of such people, but, as with leprechauns and extraterrestrials, I have not had the pleasure of personally knowing any. For most of us, a meeting is like a visit to the dentist—a lot of pain, noise, and drilling. So why dwell on the discomfort? Just look ahead to your next enjoyable event. As with preparing for a presentation, this attitude will relax you.

Outcomes of meetings get too much attention, in my opinion. Just for fun, do a little experiment sometime. Pick a project or other activity that involves a series of meetings and do some analysis. Record the outcomes, which should be directions or conclusions of importance to the project, and keep track of what happens to them. What bearing do the outcomes have on the actual efficiency of the program or its products? If you think you will find a correlation, then you will be surprised. Directions are often ignored and conclusions are frequently overturned by other events (or the next meeting in the queue). If you actually do find a correlation among meeting results and project performance, by all means try to figure out how it happened and write your own little book about it; you will have discovered something unique and valuable.

Then, given that meeting outcomes are not such a big deal anyway, our mental preparation is easy. We simply review our material and assume an attitude of contented indifference. We are going to attend, participate, and offer our wares, but what actually happens in the meeting is not a big deal because its outcomes are likely to have shorter lives and less significance than that of a fruit fly. So we can just relax, get through the meeting, and enjoy the show, which brings us to the subject of unexpected turns of events.

ANTICIPATING THE UNEXPECTED

We have talked about the unexpected in the context of meetings throughout this part of our little book, and we know that the meeting is to the unexpected as a Petri dish is to bacteria—a fertile breeding ground. Even the phrase *anticipating the unexpected* seems contradictory. How do we anticipate something we do not expect? The answer is that we do not. We do not anticipate *what* unexpected events will occur, but simply *that* they will occur. With this attitude, the unexpected is manageable.

Because we have done our planning, have the proper materials at hand, and have prepared and anticipated the environment, we are pretty confident of our ability to participate. Furthermore, because we have this attitude of confident indifference to the meeting outcomes, unanticipated events take on a new role. Let's analyze this. Unexpected events will only affect meeting outcomes (which do not matter) and we have our part of the activity well planned and prepared. Therefore, we are comfortable and participating in an activity whose outcomes are unimportant. Now, what is a good definition for an activity in which we are comfortable and whose outcome is relatively unimportant? Entertainment! And that's the key to handling unanticipated events: just treat them as entertainment, because that is precisely what they are.

We know that unexpected events will occur and that they will be entertaining. So we are ready for them. We don't know what they will be, and we don't care. Let them come about and entertain us, and we will deal with them when they do. It's as simple as that.

ZERO-PLANNING ATTITUDE ADJUSTMENTS

In a zero-planning state, we are confronted with entering a meeting with the proper attitude or, as is the case with presentations or documents, altering the attitudes of the other participants or the chairperson. The fact that some sage lacked the foresight to allow us to plan or prepare does not inhibit us in these situations, because zero planning on our part does one simple, beautiful, and wonderful thing: it increases the entertainment value of the event for everyone involved.

Let's just think about this for a minute. If we have no time to plan or prepare, yet we are required to participate in a meeting, then what are we to the others in the meeting? We are an unexpected event, that's what. Hence, we actually get to be part of the entertainment, not just observe it. This being the case, our attitude is actually elevated. We can look forward to being part of the show and providing the others with an unexpected event to deal with. So our attitude is intact. We will simply go into that meeting and be ourselves. We just do our best with what we have to work with. Additionally, we can ask silly questions, present off-the-wall ideas, and basically just enjoy being a wild card to which others must decide how to react (and if they have read this little book they will enjoy it too). Therefore, our attitude is sound and intact. Zero planning only improves the entertainment value. It is absolutely nothing to get worried about, and our attitude remains constant and confident.

In summary, we have seen that acquiring the right attitude for a meeting involves many of the same principles as other forms of communication. Physical preparation concentrating on the environment, along with the planning that precedes it, gives us a sound foundation. Mental preparation, based on the confidence wrought by planning and physical preparation, gives us the correct, confident, indifferent attitude. Preparing for the unexpected centers on treating the whole notion of a chaotic meeting as what it is—entertainment. Next, we look at how that entertainment value, along with all the other events, comes together in the dynamics of the meeting itself.

9

PARTICIPATING IN THE MEETING

In participating in the meeting, we rely even more heavily on the characteristics we use in the formal presentation: *poise, confidence,* and *dignity.* We don't get excited or engage in shouting matches, and since we have this marvelously indifferent attitude, we approach all issues coolly and objectively. We can be warm and friendly in personality, and quite cordial and cooperative. We certainly don't undergo a radical personality change if the events and decisions of the meeting do not go as we expect or desire, because we understand the true significance of meeting outcomes. We present our portion as we have prepared it, and move on. Our only expectation is that the meeting will occur, and its outcomes are merely things we may have to deal with subsequently. This is absolutely nothing to get worked up about.

However, there are a few more aspects to participating in a meeting beyond simply being there and executing our portion. These aspects are starting, interacting, and finishing.

STARTING THE MEETING

It would seem that starting the meeting should occur automatically, but the truth of the matter is that some meetings have a kind of negative inertia to them. We have this mass of people milling around a room—some seated, some standing, some walking around—and the whole thing acts just like a big bowl of jelly, wiggling around a lot yet not wanting to settle down. A competent chairperson will usually preclude this by calling everyone to their chairs, but often the chairperson seems content to just wait around while the transients recede.

At this point, if we want to get started and the group seems to be in chaos, there are a few tactics that work pretty well. One is simply to remind the chairperson that it's time to get the show on the road, so to speak. This may or may not work. A similar but stronger approach is to say to the chairperson something like, "Well, if we aren't going to start for a while, I think I will go make a few telephone calls." This can have the effect of worrying the chairperson that the crowd is going to drift away, thus motivating a call to order. Another approach is to blink the lights on and off a couple of times to indicate that something is about to happen. This also may or may not work, because some in the crowd may simply perceive this as an electrical problem. The best way is to put one of our charts on the viewer or start passing out some of our handouts, and begin discussing the material with someone. This usually works extremely well. Typically, it will draw a crowd because it looks like the meeting is getting started, but not under the chairperson's control. This usually motivates the chairperson to take over, lest control of the meeting be taken away. If not, we just continue with our material until we get the whole room involved, and make it *our* meeting. It usually will not come to this, however, because most people do not like having their meetings taken over, and the chairperson invariably will negotiate a transition from whatever we are doing into the actual meeting. At that point, we are finally getting someplace.

INTERACTING IN THE MEETING

Once the meeting starts, we get a chance to discover its dynamics. It's always good not to be the first person to speak, because the dynamics need to be analyzed for us to be effective for the duration. In the course of the first couple of discussions, we will discover many things about the meeting's dynamics, such as the following:

1. How strong a chairperson we have and whether or not he or she will be able to maintain control over the crowd or will allow interruptions from participants or outside influences such as telephone calls
2. Who the *dominators* or active participants will be— those who wish to be heard and seen and will strive to assert their positions strongly
3. Who the *passivists* or inactive participants will be— those who will just sit there with little or no desire to interact
4. Who the *participators* or genuinely interested parties are—those who will participate, ask questions, and actually care about the answers (probably a minority)

Armed with an understanding of these dynamics and these participants, and the knowledge that we probably have many variations of these personalities as well as diverse motivations for being there (as discussed in Part II for presentation attendees), we are ready for the dynamics. Once we determine the strength of the chairperson, and pick out the dominators, passivists, and participators, we are ready to play this crowd like a banjo to get the tune we want to hear.

We then do a little preliminary bridge building as the first few discussions are going on. By *bridge building,* I mean getting some liaisons going with other participants. At this point, we participate just a little bit, to gain these liaisons. For example, when a dominator is speaking, we will agree with a few of his or her points. Dominators are sometimes insecure at heart, and use their domineering styles to compensate. They also like to build empires, even in meetings, by finding kindred participants. By agreeing with a dominator, we can establish an ally for later use. Another example is when a participant or passivist is being hammered by a dominator and we come to their rescue and support their points. This gains us another ally. We might build only a few or several of these bridges, as the situation permits, but we must always do this.

Then, when we are presenting our views, we use the bridges we built to escape from problems or to guide the direction of the meeting. Now this is gamesmanship and manipulation and, in general, I prefer not to do it; rather, I prefer simply to be legitimate and straightforward. We can present our ideas and interact primarily with those who want to gain better understanding or who require our information for their own needs. In other words, we can deal mostly with legitimate participators. However, if we want a quick acknowledgment, we may fire a question like, "Don't you agree?" to a passivist, especially one with whom we have a bridge. We will typically get a positive acknowledgment. If we are being harassed by a dominator, he or she usually will not be the one with whom we have a bridge, so that cuts down on the possibilities. We can always deal with this person directly, especially if our points are indeed correct. However, if we want a rest or wish to see some good sport, we can turn to a dominator with whom we have a bridge, and say something like, "Do you see my point?" Most dominators dearly love to engage other dominators in a battle of words, so once our dominator agrees with us and opposes the one who is bugging us, we just let them have at it for a while and take a break. Generally, they will tire one another out, and we can easily slip back in and continue, much to the relief of the crowd at large.

There are lots of other ways to build bridges and use them later, and we cannot possibly cover all of them. The point here is to observe people in action, decide what category they fall into, build some bridges, and use them to our advantage as the meeting continues. Once we start doing this, we rapidly become skilled at it, and it comes almost naturally. It's not at all a difficult thing to do, as most of us are already doing it, but probably have not realized it fully. It makes the dynamics of a meeting a lot of fun, as we note the categories and test our bridge-building and using skills. We just have a good time with it.

FINISHING THE MEETING

Anything that has a start naturally will have a finish, but some meetings seem to once again have a kind of inertia and lack the ability to conclude. If the chairperson has an agenda, obviously the conclusion of the last event on the agenda should end the meeting, right? I only wish it were so simple. Some meetings go on despite being past the last topic on the agenda, whereas others are effectively over even when the agenda is not exhausted. Let's look at these two circumstances and how to deal with them.

When the last item on an agenda has transpired, *it's time to go.* If the agenda has reached completion, and the chairperson seems to be in a trance, lacking the motor skills to terminate the meeting, *we terminate it.* We just gather our materials, stand up, and say something like "Thanks for inviting me to your meeting. I have a lot of new information to take with me and digest," and head for the door. This will generally precipitate a closure by the chairperson, or at least a motion in that direction. If we want to be polite, we can linger while the chairperson formally concludes the event. But in any case the end is near.

When the meeting has evolved into a kind of sluggish, nondirectional mass, despite being only partially through the agenda, *the meeting is effectively over.* The problem is that the chairperson will almost invariably try to keep the thing afloat just because there is an agenda to follow. The symptoms of this situation are evident in the behavior of the attendees. Dominators and participators transform into passivists, passivists fall asleep, and there is a general loss of energy and lack of interest in all echelons. Nobody is asking questions, and the chairperson is only hanging on because he or she thinks that it is the honorable thing to do. At this point, we need to take action lest we be consumed by this sluggish mass. We interrupt at the next opportunity by saying something like, "This is a lot of information to digest, and I, for one, need some time to digest it. I need to break away for a while, but I could return later if I am needed."

This gives the chairperson the escape route he or she needs. The meeting can be adjourned until later, and the chairperson is not at fault; the crowd is simply saturated with all this fascinating information. Usually, the chairperson, having also perceived the demise of the event, will leap at the opportunity to break away. If not, at least *we* can escape. If the chairperson is so naive as not to see what is going on, we need to be firm in our insistence to be excused. We will usually draw support from the crowd as well. But if the chairperson and some of the crowd want to continue, so be it. If we have to stay, its creative daydreaming time; we will not be bothered with interactions or questions from the sluggish crowd.

ZERO-PREPARATION TECHNIQUES

Sometimes meetings can be just like a big vacuum cleaner: they suck you right in with no time to prepare. Once again, we can usually thank those who cannot budget time for the opportunity to participate without preparing. Under this topic in Part II, I suggested that we simply blame this situation on whoever created it and have some fun with the presentation, by becoming part of the audience and critiquing the presentation even as we are giving it. In the meeting, this is not quite so simple. Because we are interacting, not formally presenting, we may not have material to critique. Also, we may be the perfect one to be at the meeting, but without the opportunity to prepare.

Here, we call once again on our confident yet indifferent attitude, and we assume a role. Instead of the role of the entertaining critic, as with the presentation, we assume the role of the helpful expert. We can start with a statement like, "I just got pulled into this meeting and have had no time to prepare. Please apprise me of your goals for this session and the issues you are dealing with, and I will see how I can help." By approaching this situation in this manner, we accomplish three particular things. First, we show our honesty, which should be appreciated by the other participants. Second, we appear cooperative and helpful, which we are, of course. Third, we buy some time while the attendees are summarizing their meeting goals and technology, to get organized in our thinking. While listening to them, we do some of the mental preparation not afforded to us before the meeting.

Then, we ask the chairperson if we could pose a few questions before starting the planned agenda. This is usually permitted, and here we establish our role as a questioner rather than an information provider. Based on these questions, we not only gain insight into the direct issues, we also get to find the dominators, participators, and passivists in the crowd. Now that we have built our bridges, we are perceived as a questioning expert. When our time to offer something arrives, if we have some ideas, we can offer them, but I personally prefer to continue the questioning. I like to say something like, "I believe I understand the issues to be . . . (whatever)," and proceed to ask more questions. After we have asked our questions, if a position is evident, we can state it, or we can simply be honest and say that we have gained a lot of understanding but have no position or solution to offer at this time. Now the meeting continues (or ends if we are last on the agenda), and we offer to digest what we have learned and respond to the attendees later, in a memo or at a subsequent meeting

Fundamentally, what we have done is gain understanding, participate, and provide whatever we could, given the lack of preparation time. If that is not good enough, then the powers that be should allow a more reasonable time to prepare. This goes right back to the fundamental idea that quality work requires time to do it.

There is no substitute for a skilled communicator working under a reasonable schedule. When the schedule is compressed, quality gets squeezed out.

HOW TO PLAN AND CONDUCT THE MEETING YOURSELF

Now we have reached the end of Part III of our little book. But one subject we have not discussed in this part is what to do if *you* are the one who has to plan and conduct the meeting. The perspective in this part of the book has been that of the attendee, not the chairperson, and the reason is simple: nobody in their right mind wants to be the chairperson. However, if you are stuck with that task, I have some specific advice.

The steps to preparing and conducting a meeting are simple. First, buy a big book (not a little one) about how to organize and conduct meetings. Second, prepare an agenda and distribute advance copies of it to the attendees, with specific roles and responsibilities defined. Third, bring that big book to the meeting, along with more copies of the agenda, roles, and responsibilities. That is how to prepare a meeting.

When you get to the meeting room, you need to get the ball rolling. First of all, arrive on time. Then slam the big book on the table to get everyone's attention, pass out the agenda and instructions (because nobody will have read the advance copies anyway), and go for it. Keep the meeting events on time and adjourn it when it is over (actually or effectively). Now you know everything you need to know about conducting a meeting.

In summary, we have seen that we are simply applying the poise, confidence, and dignity wrought by effective planning and preparation to starting, participating in, and finishing the meeting. We have seen that the dynamics of a meeting are largely a function of the types of personalities and the nature of the chairperson, all of which we can use to our advantage once we analyze and understand them. We also have seen that we can be effective under zero-planning conditions by having the proper attitude and by applying our techniques under a somewhat more constrained situation. Finally, we have seen how to plan and conduct a meeting ourselves.

IV

CROSS-CULTURE COMMUNICATION— BRIDGING THE GAP

In the first three parts of this little book (which, by the way, is in danger of becoming a big book if I don't keep this final part short and succinct), we looked at writing, presenting, and interacting techniques and *philosophy*. For techniques, we focused upon the essentials of connection, flow, and reinforcement; and for philosophy, we outlined ways to get organized, execute the communication, and keep our attitude right and optimistic. All that information is well and good when technologists or technical managers are communicating with other technologists or technical managers—even when we cross technical area boundaries, such as biologists communicating with physicians, architects communicating with engineers, and so forth. In those earlier parts, we presented some examples and gave some advice about how to cross technical or technical–managerial boundaries, and still be effective communicators.

In our society today, technology is pervasive. It is affecting areas of our culture where, even a decade ago, it was relatively unknown. For example, we now have computer programs to assist farmers in planning crop rotation and soil treatment, often assisted by satellite or airborne remote sensing of the croplands and hyperspectral analysis of the soil content. How many farmers would we have found a decade ago who used computers, cared about anything in the sky except the clouds, sun, and moon, or had ever heard of anything called "hyperspectral?" Not many. Even in our own technical environment, we may need to communicate some information to sales people, investors, or customers who have no technical background, but still need to understand our information in their own context—*what it means to them*. The point here is that, as technical communicators, we often need to be able to provide an understanding of our technologies to audiences that are not merely nontechnical, but have completely different ways of thinking, acting, and understanding, than those we would normally communicate with.

This goes way beyond cross-technology communication or technical–management communication. It is the *undiscovered country of cross-culture communication*. The farmer wants his crops to be healthy and bountiful, and knows how to sow seeds, treat soil, and harvest. The farmer would be pleased to use any methods to assist in these chores, but does not have the time, inclination, or desire, to understand computers, remote sensing, or hyperspectral analysis. The investor wants to know how the technology will make money, and may care very little about the science or engineering that underlies the technology. In these examples, and in myriad other cases, if users are going to apply a technology, they will need to understand it *in the context of their own culture,* with its own language, methods, quirks, goals, constraints, and other peculiarities and oddities.

Our job, as communicators, is *not* to train the user to understand the technology, but to bridge the culture gap and set the technology in the user's comfortable and familiar context. How we do this—using the communication essentials from the first three parts of this book, applied to the three forms of communication: writing, presenting, and interacting—is the subject at hand. But fear not; it's easy to enter another culture and communicate. The communication essentials still work, and it is more of a *philosophical gap* we need to bridge. By the way, it can be a lot of fun as well when we do it right, as we describe in this part of our little book.

10

UNDERSTANDING A *COMMUNICATION* CULTURE GAP

Before we get into cross-culture communication techniques (for writing, presenting, or interacting), we need to have an understanding of what a communication culture gap *actually is*. We see or hear the term "culture gap" all the time, but do we really understand the basis of a culture gap, or how to work with it to achieve our goals? Once we understand this, we are ready to apply techniques to it—to overcome differences, capitalize on similarities, and communicate effectively. But first of all, let's get the horse in front of the cart right away. A *communication* culture gap exists because there is a culture gap and not the other way around. We are not different because we cannot communicate effectively. Rather, we encounter difficulties in communicating because we perceive ourselves as being different from another culture. So let's look at a couple of communication culture gaps and see what they are all about. We'll start with a fairly extreme one to make some points, then settle into a more contemporary example.

For our first example, let's say that some agricultural scientists have invented a way to increase the productivity of grapevines using a newly developed fertilizer and that they are going to promote this product to a group of Taoist monks. The scientists are accustomed to quantifying their product's worthiness in terms of plant yield efficiency, citing examples of how it has increased the productivity and profits of other clients (grape growers), and discussing how easy it is to use in conventional fertilizer-spreading apparatus. Conversely, the Taoist philosophy is that of letting things happen as they may, and going along with what Taoists call "the Way." They are just as happy with a low yield as a high one, because they believe that either case is what the Way has determined. They never think about productivity or profit, and they never plan anything. It does not matter how long it takes to sow or harvest and they are not doing it for profit anyway, but just to feed any who need sustenance. If there is not enough yield to feed all who need it, they feel that is what was supposed to happen. Finally, they use no spreading apparatus, but rather spread such products by hand. This is obviously an extreme culture gap, between capitalistic, technological agriculture and simple, nonprofit, unhurried farming.

Another example, and probably a more relevant one, is the current, and probably everlasting, debate on genetic engineering of food products. Genetic engineers have devised ways for reconstructing the genetic makeup of food products to give better growth, higher yields, and pest resistance. They like to promote their wares in terms of higher profits for growers and lower-cost, better-quality foods for consumers. However, many consumers are more concerned about health and safety issues. They want to be assured that, if they consume genetically engineered foods, they will not develop some heinous disease and that their grandchildren will not have two noses and three ears. The average consumer cannot understand genetics and until the genetic scientists address the health and safety issues *in a way that consumers will understand,* there will always be resistance to these products.

The fundamental understanding we need to gain, from analyzing these two examples or any other culture gap, consists of two aspects: (1) how we can negate troublesome differences, and (2) how we can leverage useful similarities. We can think of this situation graphically, as depicted in Figure 10.1. If we could quantify the number and significance of the similarities and differences between cultures, and plot them as a function of the magnitude of the culture gap, we would get a chart similar to the one depicted. A vertical line would then represent some actual culture gap. As Figure 10.1 shows, a large culture gap would be represented by the vertical line toward the left side of the chart, denoted as an "actual" culture gap, and would consist of many, severe differences and few, minor similarities between the two cultures. Our task as communicators is to push the line to the right sufficiently far to achieve an "effective" culture gap for communication. This culture gap, although not perfect or ideal, would consist of few, minor differences and many, signifi-

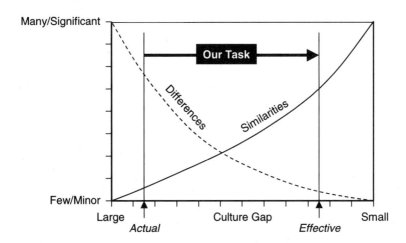

Figure 10.1 The elements of a culture gap.

127

cant similarities, which would be a workable basis for communication.

This does not mean we are *correcting* the culture gap. That's a job for politicians, disasters, saints, or the gradual changes due to time (and probably more time than we can afford to effect our communication). It means that, for the purpose of our particular communication needs, we are creating an effective culture gap that will reduce the perceptible differences and increase the perceptible similarities to the point where communication will be successful. The communicator and the recipients of the communication will *feel* that they are not so far apart. To achieve this, we must study and gain some degree of understanding of the culture we are addressing—*we have to do the homework*. For me, this is always an interesting aspect—getting to know some other culture—and when it is interesting it is also fun. Once we have a sound appreciation of the target culture, know how to recognize and negate differences, and know how to identify and leverage similarities, we are ready to set our communication techniques in the right framework to successfully bridge the cultural communication gap.

NEGATING TROUBLESOME DIFFERENCES

A good way to approach the task of understanding and negating differences is to build a three-column table, which I call a "difference–approach" table. The first column is a list of the cultural differences, the second associates a reason or basis with each difference, and the third lists an approach or maybe several candidate approaches to negate each difference. The whole table does not need to address every existing cultural difference, but only those germane to the communication goals. So a set of communication goals appears at the top of the table. Some folks try to achieve the same result—to find approaches to negate the differences—in a less formal manner. Now don't get me wrong, I am all for simplicity and the absence of formalism. However, I have found that there are usually entanglements among the difference issues that are not always apparent when one is simply concocting approaches. Culture gaps are complicated things, and not to be treated lightly. By collecting the differences, their reasons, and candidate approaches in a document, these entanglements are more easily revealed. Also, the second column (the basis or reason), is absolutely essential to success. All too often, we tend to attack a problem's symptoms and not its cause, which tends to yield an imperfect solution. Similarly, we may conceive imperfect approaches to negate differences if we do not assess the reasons for these differences. These tables are easy to prepare, so let's create a couple of them for the two agricultural examples from the first part of this chapter.

To begin, a difference–approach table for the fertilizer scientist/Taoist monk example might appear as shown in Figure 10.2. At the top, it cites the overall goal of convinc-

Communication Goal(s): (1) Convince the monks to use our fertilizer		
Differences	**Reasons or Bases**	**Candidate Approaches**
Monks do not care about yield or productivity.	Taoist philosophy of producing only what is naturally needed.	Do not push the issue - but mention how the natural increase in population has increased the need for more yield - the new fertilizer is a natural response to a natural need.
Monks do not plan or evaluate harvest.	Taoist philosophy of letting things happen as they may.	Describe how fertilizer was a natural discovery.
Monks do not use spreading machinery.	Taoist philosophy of working hard, and with simple tools.	Stress satisfaction of working the fertilizer into the soil. Describe hard work which produces the product.

Figure 10.2   A difference–approach table for the fertilizer case.

ing these monks that they should use the fertilizer. Then, in the first two columns, it identifies the cultural differences and the reasons they exist, as we described them earlier. In the third column, this communicator has decided to pose the fertilizer as a naturally evolved discovery, which fits into the natural course of events, and emphasize the hard work of the researchers who discovered it. This emphasis on natural events and hard work leading to the product's evolution is designed to appeal to the Taoist emphasis on hard work and following a natural course of events. The communicator is basically going to say that destiny and hard work has brought the product to the monks, an approach that would never work when promoting the product to a pragmatic, business-oriented commercial farming enterprise.

Next, let us take a look at the genetic engineering case, whose difference–approach table might appear as shown in Figure 10.3. In this case, the goal of convincing customers

Communication Goal(s): (1) Convince customers that genetically-engineered foods are safe		
Differences	**Reasons or Bases**	**Candidate Approaches**
Customers concerned about safety of genetically engineered foods.	Science fiction stories and movies, lack of hard evidence of safety.	Cite hard test data, or cite analogous situations in the past.
Customers suspicious of anything promoted by big business.	Track record of big businesses ignoring safety to enhance profits	Show that the genetically-engineered foods are not simply a cheap alternative - to increase food industry shareholder's profits. Explain real benefits.
Customers unschooled in science, especially genetic engineering.	Everyone cannot be a scientist or geneticist.	Explain everything through easy-to-understand analogies and metaphors, use common language and everyday terms.

Figure 10.3 A difference–approach table for the genetic engineering case.

that genetically engineered foods are safe is once again stated at the top. As in the previous example case, the first two columns list the differences and their reasons, and the third suggests some approaches to overcome the culture gap. Now this one is a difficult task, because of the element of time. In truth, it takes many generations to detect all the effects of a genetic alteration, and adequate test data simply does not exist. Similarly, over generations, many big businesses (which are not unlike big books) have consistently demonstrated a callous disregard for safety in order to increase profits. So, although the approaches listed in the third column are legitimate, they will be challenging to implement. However, implementation is the subject of later chapters, and the point here is that this mechanism—the difference–approach table—is an effective tool for bringing the differences into focus, and using an understanding of the reasons behind them to devise approaches to overcome the communication culture gap.

LEVERAGING USEFUL SIMILARITIES

Similarities between cultures, or even between the communicator and the audience, are useful tools for reducing an actual culture gap into an effective one for communication. I believe it is very useful to look for these similarities when we are analyzing the cultural differences, and incorporate them into the approaches for reducing the culture gap in the third column of the difference–approach table. A good way to do this is simply to underline the similarity aspects in the third column as well as the aspects of the reasons for the difficulty (in the second column) to which they apply. At first, I tried using a separate column for similarities, but it always seemed to have a lot of redundancy with elements of the approach column. Also, more than three columns seemed too structured for me; it was getting a bit too organized and imposing on my free-form nature of doing things. Anyone who wants to use another column should certainly do it, but I think three columns are just about right. So let us look at the two previous examples again and concentrate on the similarity aspects

Figure 10.4 repeats Figure 10.2, the Taoist monk—fertilizer product case, this time showing cultural similarities in the third column marked by <u>underlining</u>. This communicator has effectively integrated several similarities into the approaches, and the table is a good, concise summary of approaches that are likely to work when implemented in our communication techniques for writing, presenting, or interacting.

The second example case, involving genetically engineered foods, is a more difficult situation in which to find similarities, because the first two difference issues are *based on suspicion or distrust*. Think about it. If you distrust me and I say that I am similar to you, and distrust myself or what I am saying, then I am either a hypocrite or an

Communication Goal(s): (1) Convince the monks to use our fertilizer		
Differences	**Reasons or Bases**	**Candidate Approaches**
Monks do not care about yield or productivity.	Taoist philosophy of producing only what is naturally needed.	Do not push the issue - but mention how the natural increase in population has increased the need for more yield - the new fertilizer is a natural response to a natural need.
Monks do not plan or evaluate harvest.	Taoist philosophy of letting things happen as they may.	Describe how fertilizer was a natural discovery.
Monks do not use spreading machinery.	Taoist philosophy of working hard, and with simple tools.	Stress satisfaction of working the fertilizer into the soil. Describe hard work which produces the product.

Figure 10.4 A difference–approach table for the fertilizer case, with similarities marked.

idiot, and certainly not worth listening to. One tactic, which we find under the first difference item in Figure 10.5, is to show that some other, impartial, and honest entity has a similar distrust and is taking steps to monitor the activity that causes the distrust. In this case, some regulatory agency, probably the FDA, has to test and approve the process before it is used. There may also be private, nongovernment watchdog organizations that have done tests or have taken a position on the matter, which may help. So this communicator has added an item to this element of Column 3, suggesting that the foods are safe. Similarly, the second difference item in the table points out the suspicion customers may have that the genetically engineered approach exists solely to fatten the company's profit margin. So this communicator has suggested show-

Communication Goal(s): (1) Convince customers that genetically-engineered foods are safe		
Differences	**Reasons or Bases**	**Candidate Approaches**
Customers concerned about safety of genetically engineered foods.	Science fiction stories and movies, lack of hard evidence of safety.	Cite hard test data, or cite analogous situations in the past. Explain how unbiased inspections or tests ensure safety.
Customers suspicious of anything promoted by big business.	Track record of big businesses ignoring safety to enhance profits.	Show that the genetically-engineered foods are not simply a cheap alternative - to increase food industry shareholder's profits. Explain real benefits. Show substantial benefit to the customer with moderate increase in profitability.
Customers unschooled in science, especially genetic engineering.	Everyone cannot be a scientist or geneticist.	Explain everything through easy-to-understand analogies and metaphors, use common language and everyday terms.

Figure 10.5 Difference–approach table for the genetic engineering case, with similarities marked.

ing that the customer will gain (through savings) as well as the company (through profits). The similarity is that we are all capitalists and everybody likes to make a buck. It's a win–win situation for both (and this example could honestly be called fiction). Anyhow, the idea is apparent—look for similarities, think of ways to use them to reduce the communication culture gap, and annotate them on the difference–approach table, so they will be available for planning and executing the communication.

COMMUNICATING EFFECTIVELY

Now that we have examined a communication culture gap, and have a technique for analyzing it, we are almost ready to apply our communication essentials to the various types of communication that we will explore in the next three chapters. However, there are a few points of caution we need to look at before we get into communication specifics. I like to call these the "crowbars of communication." Just as a crowbar pries things apart, these mistakes will actually spread, not shrink, a communication culture gap. Learning not to do these things, whether applied to writing, presenting, or interacting, is paramount to bridging the gap and effectively communicating. So let's take a look at these communication crowbars and how they are perceived by those who are supposed to receive the communication.

Crowbar #1:   *"I'm an expert, so take my word for it."* This is the uncontested champion of ways to alienate readers or an audience. If the communicator is truly an expert, it goes without saying or is evident in the communicator's demeanor or reputation. So actually asserting this notion is generally perceived by the readers or audience in one of the following ways:

134

Perception #1a: What an egotistical jerk. This person is not worth listening to.

Perception #1b: This communicator has no knowledge and is trying to hide the fact.

Perception #1c: This communicator does not care enough about us to explain the issue.

Crowbar #2:   ***"If you want to know more about this, here are some references."*** Oh, good! Its nice to be back in high school again and get a homework assignment! This crowbar is resplendent in software "help" systems that give a list of places (often web sites) to look up your issues among ten million other issues, the whole set of which is poorly indexed, usually set in the developer's context and not the user's, and whose search system was designed by the Klingons. (In case you are not a Star Trek fan, the Klingons are an alien race who revel in confrontation and doing things by the most difficult means, for the sheer pleasure of it.) Audiences or readers will take this as follows:

Perception #2a: We do not want to wade through a bunch of references, this information is useless.

Perception #2b: What a lazy communicator. He does not even bother to explain the issues.

Crowbar # 3:   ***"This is the way we have always done it."*** Ah, yes, it's always a pleasure to be addressed by one of the last remaining dinosaurs. Don't you just love it when you hear this statement? Most readers or audiences will react to this in one of the following ways:

Perception #3a: Where did this old geezer come from? Why doesn't somebody bury him (or her)?

Perception #3b: Now I'm going to hear about something too old to be useful.

Perception #3c: This communicator is too stuck in a rut to be conveying anything useful.

There may be other, minor crowbars to watch out for as well that are peculiar to the particular audience or group of readers. However, in general, if we avoid these three main crowbars, we will avoid widening the gap, and can apply our communication essentials and techniques, as I describe in the next three chapters.

11

WRITING FOR *ANY* GROUP OF READERS

Writing for a particular group of readers is a matter of paying close attention to three aspects. The first is getting in character. We want to write for these readers as one of them, not an outsider. The second is getting back to the basics. This is where we ensure against explaining a technical subject in a manner that the readers either will not understand or will suspect is invalid. The third is staying on track. While trying to be in character and use basics, it is easy to lose our focus—much easier than when writing to a familiar group of readers about something at our particular technical level. In this chapter, we look at these three aspects, set in the context of our three communication essentials (connection, flow, and reinforcement). As usual, I also provide some tips for when you need to perform the writing without actually having the time to do it properly.

GETTING IN CHARACTER

Getting in character for writing is not unlike getting in character for a play or a musical performance. It involves not only mastery of the art (our particular technical prowess), but also an understanding of the likes and dislikes of the readers. We would not perform a symphony at a jazz festival. The instruments and notes may be the same, but the selection of music and methods of articulation are quite different. Similarly, we would not write an article about a newly developed chemical compound for users of the product in the same way we would write for a chemical engineering trade journal. The substance is the same but the selection of facts to present and the presentation techniques are different.

The way to get in character is to first do a little research and reading. If we are writing for a particular group of readers, we are most likely not the first ones in history to do so. There are always many examples of written work for any group of readers. So we simply find some of them and read them, and we do this *in the right context* as well. If we are preparing an article or column for a trade magazine, we read some articles and columns in trade magazines for the particular audience. If we are writing a book, we read books. If we are writing advertising copy, we read advertising copy. In particular, we read good examples—books, advertising copy, articles, or columns that are known to be effective and well-received by their audiences.

For example, suppose we are material scientists working for a company that makes elastic products and we have confirmed through testing that we could make large elastic bands that would replace logging chains in the lumber industry. Say that our marketing department has arranged for us to prepare an article for a logging industry trade paper. Obviously, writing for the "Paul Bunyan Times" is vastly different than preparing material for "Polymer Science Quarterly." So we read a few copies of the target publication, and see that (1) the language is mostly written in the second person, (2) the articles are usually 3–4 pages long, (3) the articles use a lot of outdoor, on-site pictures, (4) there are no descriptive diagrams, (5) there are many real-world examples of the topics cited in the articles, and (6) there are few interviews with loggers. So this tells us a lot about the style and technique in which to write, the length, the graphics, and the use of examples that will resonate with these readers. Having reviewed this material, we tell the marketing folks they had better get some samples of the product to a logging camp and take a few pictures. Then, when we design the script for our article, we apply this valuable information, thus ensuring we get a good *connection*. (Remember the connection from Chapter 1? If not, it's a *little* book—go back and read Chapter 1 again.)

An obvious aspect of this, but probably not sufficiently obvious to ignore, is that we should read *good* examples. Let's admit it—we are often lazy, and we scientists may not get much of a kick out of reading logging periodicals, but the whole idea is to get good ideas. So if the "Lumberjack News" only has a readership of 150, and "Keep On a-Loggin" has a readership of 150,000, and has won several awards, has a large advertising base, and has won glowing praise from industry sages, then the choice is obvious.

Another point worth making is not to be so scientific about this that we ignore the obvious. We scientists and engineers tend to be analytical, sometimes to a fault. When you read the example material, read it for the *feeling* as well as to analyze the contents. This is a place to get an intuitive and instinctive sense about the audience as well as to gather facts. When I read an example article for an untried group of readers, I do not make a list of the voice, person, tense, number of pictures, and so forth. I just get comfortable, read the material, and then try to do my script very soon after reviewing the material. Try it—it works.

GETTING BACK TO THE BASICS

There are two elements within the notion of getting back to the basics. The first is the obvious one. We need to set our writing at a level of understanding that the readers can follow. The second element is avoiding overuse of jargon that we do not understand and which makes us sound pretty silly if we are not careful.

Setting the right level of understanding is achieved by the research we did to get in character. This allows us to determine how we should present our information to the readers and dictates the tools we can use. We return to the elastic logging band example to examine this aspect. Recall that our research showed us that the articles are short, with lots of pictures, and no diagrams. Obviously, we are not going to use the calculations for modulus of elasticity in this article. Clearly, we are not going to put in any diagrams of atomic deformation or atomic orbital skewing. We are going to write to the basic issues of what logging chains are used for—binding and towing logs without breaking.

So we plan our article, using the script technique, to include the pictures we sent our marketing folks out to gather—pictures of elastic logging chains wrapped around huge logs being loaded, unloaded, dragged, and towed around a logging site. When composing the piece, we take a user's context and describe how to unpack, use, store, and maintain the elastic chains. We write about the elastic chains' capacity, perhaps mentioning the testing we had done in our laboratory, but concentrating on the real application, and in the logger's jargon. For example, say we had tested some prototype elastic chains of various sizes, using a set of standard weights, calibrated and traceable to the National Bureau of Standards. Should we write this?

> Scientists conducted scrupulous laboratory testing, using standard masses traceable to the National Bureau of Standards. They determined that the second-largest elastic band could elevate a weight of 5000 pounds to a height of 48 inches without exceeding the tensile strength of the material. Storage is facilitated by their relatively light weight, and maintenance can

be accomplished by a simple soap-and-water rinse, in contrast to the lubrication and rust removal required by chains.

Are you kidding? Logging magazines with words like this probably wind up as fireplace starters or outhouse accessories (and I don't mean reading material). We would write this:

> The boys in the lab tested these elastic chains using log-size weights. These babies would hoist a 36-inch, 20-foot oak log into a truck bed without snapping. When you're done with them, just rinse them off and toss them in the shed—no need for oiling or rust scraping.

The idea is to reduce the scientific language and quantification of the scientist to the necessary facts required by the user, in the form and format the reader will enjoy and relate to. In the sense of our communication essentials, this is maintaining the connection through flow and reinforcement. The flow works because the jargon is right and the reinforcement is believable because it is set at the right level of understanding.

As mentioned earlier, the second element within "getting back to the basics" lies in the art of not overusing of the readers' jargon, especially when we do not fully understand it. Let's be perfectly clear about this aspect. We scientists and technical professionals are not always "writing down" to an audience or "simplifying for the uninformed." Let's park our egos for a moment, and realize that we may often be addressing a sophisticated and intelligent group of readers whose specialty is every bit as complex and intellect-demanding as our own, just different. So when we get back to the basics, we are seeking a common ground for understanding, not a resolution of which specialty is intellectually "superior" to the other. Regardless of the relative complexity of a subject, or how much or little intelligence is involved in understanding it, if we use the basics in error, it will be obvious.

Hence, when we are attempting to use the readers' basic principles or jargon, we need to be very careful not to overuse terms we are unfamiliar with or imply an understanding we do not have. Having worked in signal processing technology for a few decades, I can cite a personal example of this. Years ago, I was part of a team that developed a method for discriminating radar signals from each other. Finding it to be a useful and accurate method, we began looking for other applications and hit upon using it to discriminate among different electrocardiogram (EKG) waveforms. We tried some test cases and it worked very well, so we wrote a proposal to a government health organization for funding to further develop and test the method. I was the lead proposal writer, and I did all the right things, up to a point. I read some medical journals and other grant proposals for this customer, prepared a script, and began writing.

Then a funny thing happened. I had become so intrigued with the elements and jargon of electrocardiography, and so enthusiastic about this application, that I started describing the purposes and elements of the EKG waveform and their significance. I was writing as if I were an expert diagnostician, having merely read a few articles. I was having a great time with the principles and the jargon, but what I was writing was completely wrong. Obviously, we did not win the grant, and the reviews from the evaluators were all alike, saying we obviously did not understand EKGs. The unfortunate thing was that the technique actually worked quite well. If I had stated early in the dissertation that we were not experts in EKG, and simply described the techniques and validity of our preliminary results, we may have had a chance. My mistake was that in getting back to the basics, I went much farther than simply trying to find common ground for communication. Rather, I tried to apply the readers' jargon without sufficient understanding. It's an easy trap to fall into, so take care to avoid it.

STAYING ON TRACK

Staying on track means accomplishing the writing task with the proper attention to connection, flow, and reinforcement, as we explained in Part 1 of this little book. All the techniques we discussed in Part 1 still apply, but there are some traps and pitfalls awaiting us when writing to an unfamiliar group of readers. The problem lies within the very things we need to do to appeal to these readers—getting in character and getting back to the basics. When we write to our familiar group of readers, within our own, comfortable specialty area, it is easy to pay the proper attention to the principles of connection, flow, and reinforcement. We know the subject matter and readers intuitively, so we are not distracted from focusing on our communication essentials by unfamiliarity with the readers. However, when we write to unfamiliar readers, we have to put extra effort into learning about and properly addressing them, which introduces distractions and uncertainty into our normal writing process. It's kind of like riding a bicycle—if you don't pay attention to where you are going, you'll bump into things; but if you go too slow, you may fall off the bike or something may run into you. However, these distractions and uncertainty problems are relatively easy to overcome, as I now explain.

Distractions often come from learning about something new and interesting as we do our reading and research to get in character. The EKG signal discrimination example earlier in this chapter is a good example of distraction—becoming so enamored with the new information that we lose our focus on the purpose of the piece we are writing or the purpose of learning the new information. Another example of a distraction would be an architect learning about the needs of a law school for a new administration building, and then including advice about how to administrate student loans in a proposal for designing the building. A common distraction comes when

143

technologists become involved with sales or marketing people. The purpose of the write-up is usually to describe how a technology can serve a market, but technologists often get wrapped up in the money issues and include advice about how to price the product. All these things fall under the category of "happens often and rarely works well."

We have mechanisms readily available to us to avoid distractions such as these. The first one is the *script* described in Chapter 1, and the second one is the *difference–approach table* described in Chapter 10. As Figure 11.1 illustrates, these mechanisms provide the guidance and structure necessary to keep us on the right track in our

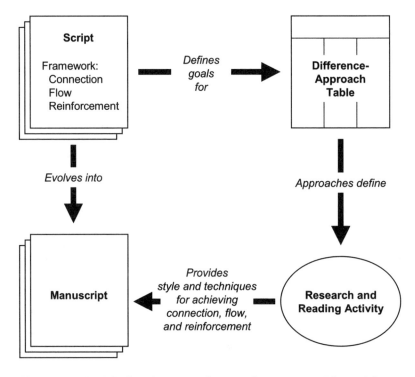

Figure 11.1 Mechanisms work together to provide guidance and structure for document planning.

document planning and writing. Recall from Chapters 1 and 3 that the purpose of a script is to define the connection, flow, and reinforcement necessary to effectively perform the writing and create a manuscript. We actually write directly into the script, and it evolves into the manuscript. The script will also define the communication goals that we put into our difference–approach table. In other words, we have communication goals because there is some connection, flow, and reinforcement we wish to achieve in our document, and we have a communication culture gap (cultural differences) to overcome due to the nature of the readers. So we prepare the script and difference–approach table before we embark on any research or reading activity that will reveal the style and techniques we can use to overcome the culture gap and achieve the connection, flow, and reinforcement demanded by our script.

The key is to stay focused on the script and the difference–approach table, while doing our research and reading activity to understand the targeted readers. As we read into the subject matter of the targeted readership, we simply ask ourselves two questions:

1. How will this information achieve my approaches to negate communication culture gap differences from the difference–approach table?
2. How will this information assist the connection, flow, and reinforcement my script requires?

Then, as each piece of outside material is digested, we can include the information it reveals into the script along with a note regarding how it negates some cultural difference. The technique and style information simply become components of the script so that we maintain a good focus and stay on track while evolving the manuscript from the script.

Uncertainty comes from overworrying about misuse of some of the jargon or techniques we pick up from reading applicable material for a new group of readers. It is the flip-side of overusing new material, basically being too timid or conservative because we don't want to write something inappropriate or silly. Uncertainty can cause us to fall short in our attempts to get in character for our writing, and leave the communication culture gap wider than it should be.

I don't believe there is an absolute rule for avoiding uncertainty. It is a very individual thing, peculiar to each writer, the written work, and the readers being targeted. However, my advice is to do three things to the degree you are comfortable with them:

1. Check the accuracy of what you are writing. This can be done through more research or through an early review of your work prior to publication by someone knowledgable in the subject area.
2. Let the publication's reviewers catch the problems. Most written work will go through some kind of editorial review. Trade magazines and journals do not want their articles to appear out-of-touch any more than the author does. However, if you are going to rely heavily on this step, make sure the reviewers themselves are qualified to catch problems.
3. If you are going to err, do it on the aggressive side. This is a personal opinion, but I think most readers will be more forgiving of a few mistakes in jargon than they will of an out-of-touch work. Also, even if the jargon is a bit off occasionally, its use (even misuse) at least says to the readers that this author cared enough to attempt to be in character. I think most readers appreciate the effort.

So we see that the solution to distractions and uncertainty lies in maintaining focus on the script and the difference–approach table, and achieving the proper amount of confidence in our command of the new knowledge we have gained. It is basically a balance problem—stay focused on the communication goals and try to hit the right level of being in character.

ZERO-TIME TECHNIQUES

Now this aspect of writing to an unfamiliar group of readers seems rather daunting, doesn't it? In Chapter 1, I said that a good way to *plan* a document with no time to do it was to derive it from an existing, similar one. But we probably do not have a good, similar one for an unfamiliar group of readers. In Chapter 2, I suggested that adopting a casual and indifferent attitude, and basically enjoying the writing purely for its entertainment value, would be effective in preparing to write with little or no time to do it. This is still a good tactic, regardless of the subject matter or audience. Chapter 3 was about actually doing the writing, and the zero-time technique was to basically scale the piece to the time allocated to writing it, omitting detail that would take too long to include. But it is difficult to scale a piece for an unfamiliar audience, especially without the time to do the research.

So it looks like two of our zero-time techniques, for planning and writing, will not be quite as effective here, basically due to the unfamiliarity factor. It's a good thing that the attitude trick still works, because we *really* need a good attitude to get past this obstacle.

The solution to planning and writing a piece for an unfamiliar audience, without time to research the piece adequately and without time to write it well, is to take one step beyond getting back to the basics and get back to the extreme basics. We research a piece for an unfamiliar audience to understand their world. So if we do not have time to do this, we find a world we both already live in, a place where the communication culture gap does not exist, so we do not have to plan a way to overcome it. We may be polymer scientists and our audience may be lumberjacks, but we all go to the grocery, buy gas, see movies, have meals, raise children, and do many more similar things. Hence, we plan our document to use metaphors and examples common to all, so we can write about it and the audience can relate to it without our having to do the research and reading.

For example, if we were information technologists preparing a written piece for a gardening journal, we might plan to use a grocery store example, since it, like IT, requires good organization, indexing, and access. Having planned to use the grocery store metaphor, we would then plan the places in our script where we would apply it (such as in the introduction, to set the tone, and other strategic places in the article). Then, in a second script, we might write our introduction something like this:

> Information technology (IT) helps us all in many ways. We can think of IT as a well-organized grocery store, with everything in a sensible place, clear signs on all the aisles telling us where to find things, and wide, clutter-free aisles to let us get to the grocery items we are looking for. IT simply puts all our information in sensible places in what we call a *database*. It also tells us where to find things, through what we call an *indexing system*, and provides a means to get to the information we are looking for using something called a *search strategy*. In this article, we will explore the benefits and uses of IT, for applications from grocery lists to gardening.

Then we would complete the article, using the grocery store or other common, everyday, and well-known situations as examples, while frequently alluding to the similarity between our general examples and gardening aspects.

In the case of writing the document, we simply ignore the fact that there may be different levels of elaboration. We just use the most basic level, period. This keeps us away from using too much of our jargon and expertise, or misusing the audience's jargon and specialized knowledge. We strike the balance between distraction and uncertainty by moving to such a basic level that there is no distraction or uncertainty. It is not as effective as properly getting in character and using the audience's terms and knowledge, but it will work reasonably well and can be done quickly and without research. Here's an example, continuing the grocery store–IT tactic:

> One search strategy in a database is called a *tree search*. Now, this has nothing to do with horticulture, but simply implies that different branches of the tree contain certain types of items. We do tree searches every time we go to the grocery. One branch of our grocery store tree could be frozen foods, another could be produce, and yet another could be baking supplies. When we go to the grocery, we do not look for each item in every aisle. Rather, we look for carrots in the produce area, ice cream in the frozen foods area, and flour in the baking supplies area. Similarly, the tree search in a database does not look for each item of interest in every part of the database. Items are categorized into their tree branches and the search strategy looks for the right items in the right places. So a database of gardening supplies or seeds will be accurately searched with speed and efficiency.

In summary, this chapter has brought out some ways to overcome a communications culture gap. We have seen how to get in character, get back to the basics, stay on track, and how to accomplish these things with no time to accomplish them. Using these technique, coupled with the communication essentials we described in Part I, will allow anyone to write effectively for any audience.

12

PRESENTING TO
ANY AUDIENCE

Presenting a talk or briefing to an unfamiliar audience has many similarities to writing for an unknown group of readers. We still need to get in character and get back to the basics, and we still need to negate culture gap differences and take advantage of similarities. This means we need to do a lot of the same kind of preparation, or homework, that we would do if we were planning a written piece. The main difference lies in the delivery technique. As we pointed out in Part II, when we move from a written work to a presentation mode, we are now right in front of the audience, and subject to immediate feedback. Bearing this in mind, the keys to successfully addressing an unfamiliar audience lie in three areas: (1) planning for the unknown, (2) getting acquainted, and (3) keeping together with the audience, all the while attending to our basic communication essentials (connection, flow, and reinforcement). In this chapter, we will explore tricks and techniques to successfully navigate these three areas, and also learn methods for getting ready for a presentation to an unfamiliar audience with little or no time to do it.

PLANNING FOR THE UNKNOWN

The first step in planning a presentation for an unfamiliar audience is to analyze the audience–presenter relationship. We need to know the audience we are going to be addressing, and how they interact with speakers, as well as possible. This is only common sense and applies to familiar audiences as well, except that we typically already understand familiar audiences, the ones we address routinely in the course of our work.

A good way to gain an understanding of an unfamiliar audience and how they interact with presenters is to visit a similar presentation or symposium. This not may always be possible, but when it is, *be sure to take advantage of it.* In some cases, when we cannot personally attend, there may be videotapes of the event or conference proceedings we can obtain and review. These items are not as good as being there, but are helpful in a limited way.

If we attend a similar event, we are not there to enjoy the refreshments or to chat with our companions. We are there to understand the audience–presenter interaction. This means understanding every aspect of the presentation and the audience, and not merely the blatant, obvious issues within the presentation. To accomplish this, we need to divide our attention among the presentation, the presenter, and the audience, and understand certain key aspects of their characteristics and behavior, as Figure 12.1 illustrates. Below, we list some things we need to observe and understand.

Understanding the Presentation. When observing the presentation, we look for the typical "chartsmanship" elements: style, balance of graphics and textual information, types of graphics (drawings, diagrams, photographs, or charts), type of text, complexity of the charts themselves, whether or not animation is used, and choice of color combinations (complementary, contrasting, vivid, or soft). While observing and noting these aspects of the presentation, we should also observe which types of presenta-

152

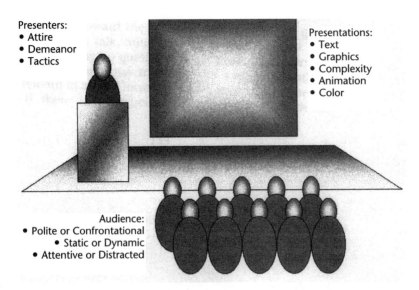

Figure 12.1 Division of attention among the presenter, the presentation, and the audience.

tions seem to be most appreciated by the audience. This is indicated by the relative alertness or drowsiness of the audience, and the amount and kinds of questions they offer.

Understanding the Presenter. We need to analyze the presenter personalities, and see which ones seem to "grab" the audience best. First of all, pay attention to their attire. Is it casual or formal or somewhere in between? Then, observe their demeanor and tactics. Which ones are most effective? Some presenters may stick to the charts closely, whereas others may let the audience read the charts while they add information with their talk. Some may point a lot at specific chart items, others may gesture occasionally and generally toward the screen. Some may solicit questions during the talk, others may wait until the end, and others may allow no questions at all. Some presenters are very animated and may move around a lot, while others may remain in a fixed location (which is sometimes necessary if there is no wireless or long-cord microphone setup). We know from Chapter 6 how a good presenter uses three attributes—poise, confidence, and dignity—to execute an effective presentation. Careful observation of the reactions of the unfamiliar audience to the presenters will reveal what particular spins on these attributes are most effective for this kind of audience.

Understanding the Audience. Having observed the presentation and the presenter, our final focus is on the audience itself, not so much how they react to the presentation and the presenter—we should have already observed these aspects in analyzing the presentation and the presenter—but on the behavior or demeanor of the audience. As you observe the audience, ask yourself some questions. Are they polite, offering reasonable questions and accepting answers gracefully? Or are they confrontational, trying to start arguments and interrupting a lot? Do they throw things? You should avoid presentations to audiences that require a bullet-proof glass shield for the presenter. Is there a lot of moving about, such as people entering and exiting the room, or is the audience fairly static? Are they attentive or do they talk among themselves a lot?

By answering these questions, we can get a notion of how this kind of an audience will react to us as presenters, regardless of the subject matter. It will also allow us to set our expectations and plan for the presentation. Polite audiences are easy to deal with. Confrontational ones will require us to respond to interruptions and will make it more difficult to maintain control. Audiences that move around or talk a lot will lack attentiveness, and it will be more challenging to keep our connection and flow going when we do the presentation.

If we cannot attend a similar presentation to a representative audience, we can look at proceedings or perhaps view videotapes. However, proceedings will only help us understand the presentation and videotapes typically focus on the presenter. So these assets will fall short of allowing us to understand the audience. When this is the case, a good tactic is to contact a few of the presenters of a similar symposium, and ask them some of our questions regarding the audience. Typically, presenters are sympathetic to other presenters (kind of a brotherhood under fire), and are happy to share their knowledge.

Having analyzed the presenter, presentation, and audience, we use this information to plan our presentation, using the planning techniques we described in Chapter 4. We apply the results of our research into the audience's specialty area to be in character and get back to the basics, just as we would for a written piece, and incorporate this information into our presentation script. We use our understanding of the presentation to design our charts, and our understanding of what constitutes an effective presentation to plan our talk and timing. We apply our understanding of the audience to ensure that our connection and flow will be intact, and this may require some additional reminder charts for an audience that we expect to be somewhat inattentive. Then, with the right preparation and attitude (which we cultivate as we described in Chapter 5 and which is no different for an unfamiliar audience), we are ready to perform.

GETTING ACQUAINTED

Once we have analyzed presenter, presentation, and audience, have prepared, and have the right attitude, we are ready for the event. But for an unfamiliar audience, unlike a familiar one, we need to get acquainted. This is the icebreaker; we do some preparation ahead of the event and then accomplish this while our title chart is in front of the audience. When we first get in front of the audience, to get acquainted, we want to interact personally, with no special supporting charts. Basically, we want the audience's attention on us and not a visual aid. Typically, this is where we have the audience's best attention, since the last presenter has concluded, and we are now something new that has popped up. Our goal is twofold: (1) to supplement our presentation with anything peculiar to this particular audience, and (2) to become one of the group and not an outsider.

Supplementing the Presentation. This activity begins before we reach the point of our presentation. Even if we have done all the planning we can, there will still be something about this audience that is different than any we may have observed to do our planning. Or, we may not have had the opportunity to attend any similar events to assist us in our planning. That's life—full of surprises and unexpected happenings. So when we arrive at the event, we must expect to do some on-the-spot research to supplement our plans.

If the event has many presentations, and ours is not the first one, we can observe other presentations and gain valuable insights. Here, we look for the same kinds of things we would look for if we were observing the event to do the planning. The only difference is that we have already done the planning and created the presentation. So our thoughts at this point are not on how to plan, but how to adapt what we already have, based on this new information we are getting. Although we cannot change our charts at this point, we can decide which points and which charts are best suited to the event and decide how to emphasize or bypass certain elements. Although we cannot change our attire drastically, we can make some simple alterations, such as removing our jacket or loosening or removing our tie. When in doubt, always overdress. We can easily dress down by removing things, but we cannot easily dress up by adding things we do not bring. Although we cannot change what we have prepared based on earlier assumptions about the audience, we can adjust our presentation style on-the-fly, to adapt ourselves to what this audience seems to like. If we have the right attitude (and we certainly do if we read Chapter 5), this can all be a great game—figuring out how to adapt yourself on the spot.

Here is an example. Imagine that we are electronic engineers giving a talk to a marketing association about how our new Wonderwidget model 427 cellular telephone reduces in-call static and automatically dials any person you want, just by saying their name. Assume also that we have attended what we believed was a similar marketing seminar, and noted that all the presentations focused on marketing issues (reducing cost, improving production speed, reaching more customers). So we arrive at the event, with a bunch of charts crammed full of marketing and sales data, and listen to the first few talks. But what's this? Every talk is receiving technical questions from the audience. There are a *bunch of engineers* in the audience. These are either engineers whose companies have decided need marketing exposure or some that have succumbed to the dark side and become marketers themselves. But the bottom line is that they are going to ask questions for which we have prepared no charts.

So what? We can overcome this difficulty, and we make ourselves some notes about technical performance and specifications. Then, when we arrive at the podium, we adopt one of two tactics. The first one is to begin our talk by saying that although the charts focus on marketing issues, we will be commenting on the technical specifications throughout the talk. The second one is simply to drag the talk out so long that there is no time for questions. That's easy, isn't it? And it is a good piece of advice in general—always have the ability to run long and avoid the question session. This can save you on many occasions. Use this tactic if you can't remember the technical specifications, or more generally if you cannot compensate for the shortcoming you have discovered, or if you simply are not in the mood for a bunch of nit-picking technical questions.

If we happen to be the first presenter, or perhaps the only presenter, we obviously cannot observe other presentations at the event. But we can do the next best thing, which is to get in touch with the event organizers before the event or to arrive early and chat a bit with the audience and the event organizers. Event organizers in particular do not want their events to fail, so they will be more than happy to answer any questions we may have. We take a direct and honest approach, and ask the questions we need to have answered about the audience and the best way to reach them. Then we move forward with poise, dignity, and confidence.

Becoming One of the Group. Becoming one of the group is something we have to do immediately upon reaching the podium. If we have successfully gone through the "getting acquainted" stage, we will either have observed other presentations, talked to some of the organizers, or met some of the audience. Any of these activities will yield information we need to "break the ice," so to speak. Here are some examples of what we may have learned and how to use it.

Our observation of earlier, well-received presentations may have revealed certain key aspects of interest. We can mention these in our opening remarks and allude to how our topic relates to them. In other words, we become one of the group by association with something the group holds as important and relevant.

Similarly, in a prior presentation or two, we may have observed a predominant mention of some industry experts and their positions on certain topics. We can mention how our topic relates to these individuals' positions. We become one of the group by associating our material with that of respected members of the group. When using this tactic, we avoid being too specific. For example, say that Dr. Frank Jones is an expert in cellular telephone noise reduction. We would mention that our Wonderwidget model 427 is designed to abate static, which may be one of the noise problems Dr. Jones is concerned with. However, we would not say that our techniques are better or equal to Dr. Jones' methods or that we are addressing the same, precise noise aspects. We want to appear to be working on the same problem as Dr. Jones, but not appear to be competitive or redundant to Dr. Jones' work.

Other opportunities to appear part of the group might include working for the same customers as group members, using the same resources or supplies as group members, being affected by similar government regulations as group members, and many others too numerous to list here. The basic point is that we should open our talk with the kinds of remarks that capitalize on significant similarities and make the audience feel that we are one of their crowd. It will really make the rest of the presentation go much smoother. It's a two-way benefit—the audience will be generally more receptive and attentive, and the presenter will feel more at ease.

KEEPING TOGETHER

Given that we have planned for the unknown and successfully become acquainted with the audience, we are ready to proceed through the presentation. In this mode, we are highly susceptible to losing the audience's attention, much more so than when presenting to a familiar audience. Even if we have done all our homework properly, analyzed the audience, prepared perfect charts, and successfully been accepted as one of the group in our opening remarks, this is still an unfamiliar audience. They are extremely easy to lose with even the slightest diversion from their particular interests.

A good way to keep the audience with us is to periodically do something a little bit unusual. Hollywood does this kind of thing in movies with a "running gag." This is something, usually not particularly germane to the plot, that recurs frequently. The audience tends to pay close attention, just to catch the next occurrence of the action. In our case, we want to do something subtle, not set the stage curtains on fire or push the podium over. One tactic is to keep moving an object around the stage. For example, maybe the facility has provided a glass of water for the speakers. After a few charts into the briefing, we take the glass of water and set it at the corner of the stage, without mentioning it in what we are saying. Later on, maybe we pick it up and move it somewhere else. Still later, maybe we pick it up, look around, then put it back where we got it. These little things will keep the audience wondering, and a curious audience is an attentive one.

If there are no objects available, we can at least count on having a screen and a pointer. We can point occasionally to a corner of the screen, for no particular reason. Or maybe trace some imaginary pattern on the corners of the screen every few charts. The key is to be interesting but not obnoxious, and it will keep the audience alert.

Sometimes these antics will precipitate a question from the audience, such as "What was all that business with the glass of water?" or "What were you pointing at on the screen?" Just tell them that it is a little ritual you picked up and do for good luck, or say that it just something you do to keep focused. Be a little mysterious— they'll come back and listen to you again.

ZERO-PLANNING TECHNIQUES

Well, this should be an interesting section, shouldn't it? Just about everything we talked about in this chapter relies on preparation time. We want to visit similar events to plan for the unknown, and we want to arrive early enough at our event to view other presentations, or to talk to organizers or attendees to get acquainted. So how do we operate successfully if we have no time for any of this? We have all seen this kind of situation. Basically, the boss calls you at 1:30 and tells you to get over to the local auditorium and give the Farmer's Guild a half-hour talk on the Wonderwidget model 427. We barely have time to gather some existing briefing material together and get there, much less to plan or observe. What do we do?

Simple, we turn the half-hour talk into a 20-minute talk, and use the first 10 minutes to plan and get acquainted. Honesty and directness are our allies here (we have no time for deception or lengthy approaches here, even if we wanted to use such tactics, which we do not). A good method is to introduce ourselves, state why we are here, and admit right up front that we haven't a clue exactly why our topic would be of interest to the group. Then, we start questioning the audience in a friendly and cooperative way. It is helpful to have the auditorium lights turned up at this point, so we and the audience can see each other. We might ask questions like "How do you farmers use cellular telephones now?" or "What problems are you having with your cellular phones." Then, we mentally note their answers, all the while analyzing their demeanor and style of language. When we have enough material to get started, we can start showing a few charts, verbally making the connection to the needs the audience stated in the questioning session.

But what if nobody offers an answer to the questions? Well, it can get kind of embarrassing standing there asking a bunch of questions and getting no answers, but this rarely happens. We can count on getting at least a few answers. If the answers are sparse and unrevealing, the best technique is then to say something like, "Well, I'll tell you a few things about how the Wonderwidget has helped other cellular phone users." and then start going through the charts, moving slowly and explaining everything at the most basic level. In this manner, although we may not be hitting the audience's hot buttons, we at least are not confusing them. It is usually not necessary to use tactics for keeping together with the audience, such as the trick of moving objects around, in this situation. By admitting we are new to this world, and questioning the audience, we already appear to be a fairly strange character, and the questioning has killed off about one-third of our time. So we do not have to hold their attention for very long. If the audience has answered some questions, we probably have their interest, and if not, they are probably looking forward to seeing us squirm around and try to compensate.

161

In either case, we have their attention, and our mastery of poise, confidence, and dignity (from Chapter 6) will keep us from appearing exceptionally foolish. Its all in good fun, anyway.

To summarize this chapter, now we see how to plan for the unknown, get acquainted with our audience, and keep the whole thing together. Remember what we talked about in Chapter 5, maintain that healthy, positive, indifferent attitude, and just have fun with the whole thing. Now we are ready to move from the unknown into the unbelievable—meeting with an unfamiliar group—which is the subject of our next chapter.

13

MEETING WITH *ANYONE* OR *ANY* GROUP

As with presenting to an unfamiliar audience, meeting with an unfamiliar group has a lot of similarities to writing for an unknown group of readers. Once again, we need to get in character and get back to the basics, and we must strive to negate culture gap differences and take advantage of similarities. Once again, we must do the same kind of preparation we would do if we were planning a written piece. In meeting with an unfamiliar group, the primary difference from the written piece is that we will get immediate feedback, and the difference between meeting with a group and presenting to an audience is that we will have less control over the whole situation, and will be doing much more interaction than we would for a presentation to an audience. These aspects are nothing new, and we pointed out the same kinds of issues in Part III.

The real difficulty lies in the unfamiliarity. If we were meeting with a familiar group, we would know their quirks, jargon, behavior, and other attributes that we could use to plan and participate in the meeting, using the techniques we described in Chapters 7 and 9. The unfamiliar group has such attributes too; we just don't know about them. So our challenge is to fit into the situation despite these differences. It is, once again, a matter of overcoming the culture gap, but doing so in a highly interactive environment. The keys to success consist of preparation, making the group comfortable with us, making the whole encounter enjoyable, not confrontational, and knowing ways to succeed with little or no time to prepare, as I describe in the remainder of this chapter.

PREPARING FOR THE ENCOUNTER

Preparing for a meeting with an unknown group is similar to preparing to write or preparing to present, but more constrained. All groups do not necessarily have web pages, or publish literature. If the group we are meeting with does, that's great, and we can research these published works and use the tactics from Chapter 11 to get in character, perhaps using the difference–approach table to organize our thinking on how to overcome the communication culture gap. All groups do not necessarily open their meetings to the public either. If our anticipated group does, that's good, and we can perhaps visit one or two of their meetings to learn about them, and then apply the techniques from Chapter 12 to get in character. Realistically, though, we may not be able to read much background material or attend similar meetings in order to prepare. So what do we do on these occasions? Once again we rely on getting back to the basics, as we introduced in Chapter 11, for writing to a group of unfamiliar readers.

In preparing for the meeting, we list all the things we know about the group, albeit this may be very little, as we just discussed. However, even the most private group on earth will have some attributes that are known. For example, we will know the time and place of the meeting—we have to know that much just to get there on time. We will

164

most likely know the subject of the meeting, otherwise why would we be going in the first place? We may also be able to discover information about the group's composition, their age spans, their gender makeup, or their interests. (The name of the group will usually give this away; the "East Side Rod and Gun Club" just *may* be interested in hunting and fishing—just a wild guess). So we think about those aspects, and any others we may ferret out, and how we might tie our expertise to such general information, in a very basic way. We basically have to do some detective work—make some assumptions and formulate some deductions based on the facts that we have.

Here's an example. Let's say we are information technology experts attending a Tuesday afternoon meeting of a package-distribution supervisor's organization at a distribution company's conference room to learn about how they control and track inventory and to discuss how our data mining (database search and retrieval) software could help them automate their control and tracking endeavors. First, we can list what we know about the group and how that relates to what we wish to communicate:

Known about Group:	Relationships to Communication
Supervisors	These are probably more senior people, as opposed to junior staff. However, they may be unfamiliar with newer database management techniques or data mining. We should plan how to deliver a short and succinct introduction to data mining.
Meets on Tuesday afternoon	Since they are allowed to meet on company time, the participating companies must see this as a valuable interchange, making it a good place to promote our product. We should plan to stick pretty much to business issues.
Meets in conference room	The ability to coordinate a meeting of selected individuals at a single location, with participants from all over the

	region, is similar to sorting and retrieving data in a data mining system. We may be able to use this metaphor.
Location is at an airport	This company has located at an airport, probably to facilitate the physical transfer of packages between the air carriers and the ground transport system. This is analogous to deciding what kind of database system to employ for accessing and distributing data. This is another good metaphor we can use.
Package distribution context	They are accustomed to dealing with a practical organization of items. Any discussions on sorting, storing, and retrieving should be easily understood.
Control and tracking needs	They have to label and track physical items in a distributed system. Discussions about tagging and tracking data items in a distributed database will be analogous and easily understood.

The point here is that we can develop a good understanding of a group from a fairly minimal amount of information. As the example above illustrates, from a bare minimum of information, we were able to accomplish the following:

1. Anticipate the knowledge level of the group about our particular subject.
2. See that the group meeting is important to the participating companies; it is a venue that is more business-oriented than social.
3. Come up with two good metaphors for our participation in the discussions.
4. Discover two useful analogies between our subject and their endeavors.

We derived all of this from merely knowing when, where, and who we were meeting with, and the subject of the meeting. Sherlock Holmes can do it and so can we.

Now armed with this understanding, to complete our planning we use the meeting preparation techniques of Chapter 7, perhaps supplemented by a culture gap analysis using our difference–approach table from Chapter 11 as an aid. However, we must keep in mind that a meeting is not as well-structured as a written piece or a presentation, and we are not necessarily in control. So the less structured and more flexible we are in our planning, the better off we will be.

GENERATING COMFORT

Once we arrive at the meeting, having accomplished our planning as described above, our first step is to get the group comfortable with us. All of the preparation we have done, and the ability to use our connection, flow, and reinforcement techniques, will be of little use if there is no feeling of comfort. Generating comfort has to do with *fitting in without appearing to be trying too hard to fit in.* Now that is just a tongue-twisting way of stating a simple concept—be yourself, but be observant and use the observations to adapt to the situation.

The best way to do this is *not* to do some kind of role-playing. Unless you happen to be an accomplished actor who can observe a situation and get into character immediately, it will come off as insincerity (or just plain foolishness). Rather, be an honest, interested, and curious guest. There will probably be some time to get acquainted with some of the participants before the meeting actually starts. This is a good time to introduce ourselves and ask a few questions about the group's focus and intentions for the meeting. We want to do this in a noninterrogative way. We want to let our natural curiosity come through, as an interested guest. That will endear us to the group. We do not want to act like reporters or detectives. That will distance us from the group, unless, of course, it happens to be a meeting of reporters or detectives. Then we can be as openly nosey, interrogative, and prying as we want, and everyone will think that is just fine.

When the meeting starts, we can hopefully remain quiet for a time and observe the dynamics. For the familiar audience, in Chapter 9, in the early stages of a meeting or before it formally starts, I suggested sorting out the dominators, passivists, and participants. This knowledge allowed us to make liaisons (bridges) and plan how to interact. For the unfamiliar audience, these types of personalities will also be apparent, and knowing this will help us navigate the meeting. However, I would not suggest trying to build bridges with members of an unfamiliar group. We simply are not savvy enough to do this well in an unfamiliar setting. It's kind of like fishing with a small line and tackle in unfamiliar waters. If a really big fish bites, we may not be able to handle it, and a really big one might sink the boat. Better to keep the line out of the water and just enjoy the ride when in an unfamiliar pond.

Once we know the group dynamics, we can start participating, always gently and with tact, and never attempting to dominate or take over an unfamiliar meeting. It is most useful to use any analogies or metaphors we may have uncovered in the preparation stage to make our entry into the discussions. This is a good technique to get our connection going. For instance, continuing the example we used earlier, for an information technologist attending a package-distribution supervisors meeting, we might take a cue from one of the participants who happens to mention the difficulty he or she had getting through cross-town traffic to get to the meeting. This is an entry point for us, and we might say something like this: "You know, navigating traffic is not unlike your job of controlling package transfer, and it has a lot to do with the volume and the route planning. Data mining is a lot like that as well, and we are always confronted with avoiding bottlenecks, for different volume conditions, with different start and destination points." And then we could begin a discussion about how the data mining software automatically avoids problems in moving and tracking items in the system. We have auspiciously and gently woven our first thoughts into the fabric of the meeting. Now we are part of the group and may proceed.

In other words, generating comfort is largely a matter of slipping smoothly and unobtrusively into the group, and then entering the conversation in ways that make easily understood transitions from the topic at hand into our subject. In a more formal or structured meeting, we may be asked to talk when our turn comes, rather than entering the discussion at will. In these cases, we just make some notes of the entry points as they occur in others' comments and use them when our turn arrives. If we are asked to speak first, we use whatever information we may have gleaned from premeeting conversations, or ask a question or two about the group's business or interests that day, to give us our entry information. The key is to make the connection between our subject and their interests effortlessly, and then add reinforcement information when we have their attention.

MAKING IT ENJOYABLE FOR EVERYONE

Now that we have prepared for the meeting and are successfully making connections and generating comfort along the way, a final aspect we need to watch carefully is to ensure that everyone is having a good time. This does not imply that we become social directors. Also, we do not have absolute control over this aspect, as the group's participants may already be confrontational, argumentative, or just plain mean and nasty. That is not our problem and, in point of fact, may even work to our benefit.

Our position is that of a guest, and most groups will not want to embarrass themselves in front of a guest. So an argumentative group may refrain from their usual confrontational behavior while we are there, even if that is their typical style. At any rate, our position is not to take

169

sides or resolve confrontations. Rather, when we participate, we want to be positive, friendly, and straightforward. If the rest of the group is already that way, we will simply fit in all the better. If not, we will seem like a breath of fresh air when we are talking, since we are not part of any confrontation that may surface.

Going a step further, we can always enhance the enjoyability of an occasion by being passively friendly, open, honest, and upbeat. We should avoid troublesome or depressing side-excursions, even if some tragic event is current and newsworthy. Don't go into some meeting and talk about a recent tragedy. Even when it is newsworthy, such a topic will cast a pall upon the event if it gets in control. We can take a good lesson from those Taoist monks we talked about in Chapter 10. Our best posture is to let the meeting go as it will, not trying to influence either its direction or outcome, and simply offer our information for what it is worth in a positive and understandable way.

ZERO-PREPARATION TECHNIQUES

The best technique for participating in a meeting for which we have no time to prepare is to avoid it. Now is a good time to go back and read the meeting avoidance and meeting filtering techniques in Chapter 7. These are good methods and they work well with familiar audiences, since we understand the meeting and the attendees well enough to gracefully challenge the invitation we have been given. For meetings with unfamiliar audiences, we can add one more technique to our little bag of tricks— make the wrong impression so that they think we might be dangerous. Assume we are an architect who specializes in office building design, and our supervisor, who wants everyone in the organization to go forth and tout the virtues of the company, has asked us to talk about our designs to a group of pharmaceutical company executives that afternoon. Our response to this request would go something like this:

"That sounds like a good idea, boss. These drug companies are expanding rapidly these days, and will certainly need new office buildings. You know, I have always wanted to meet with these people, and ask them how they can get away with some of their tactics. I would have difficulty sleeping at night knowing I was making such grand profits while people who could not afford my products were being driven into poverty. And the testing aspect of their business is curious also. We have to endure many kinds of inspections and adhere to many regulations when we design a building, but these drug companies seem to be able to skip over their regulations and avoid punishment when they release something that harms its users. Yes, I would really enjoy questioning these people. But, you know, I am pretty busy with Project X, and it will be difficult to get away to do this right now."

Do you see what we have done? Let's analyze it part-by-part:

Step 1: Agree to do it	"That sounds like a good idea, boss. These drug companies are expanding rapidly these days, and will certainly need new office buildings."
Step 2. Plant the seed of dissent	"You know, I have always wanted to meet with these people and ask them how they can get away with some of their tactics."
Step 3. Suggest an ethical problem	"I would have difficulty sleeping at night knowing I was making such grand profits while people who could not afford my products were being driven into poverty."
Step 4. Suggest legal issues	"And the testing aspect of their business is curious also. We have to endure many kinds of inspections and adhere to many regulations when we design a building, but these drug companies

	seem to be able to skip over their regulations and avoid punishment when they release something that harms its users."
Step 5. Imply confrontation	"Yes, I would really enjoy *questioning* these people."
Step 6. Offer a way out	"But, you know, I am pretty busy with Project X, and it will be difficult to get away to do this right now."

Do you see what we have done. The boss wants us to talk to these people to impress them with our architectural capabilities, and hopefully drum up some new business for the firm. Our response to the request indicates that we are happy and agreeable to attend the meeting, but we have dissenting views, disagree with the group's ethical and legal tactics, and are planning to confront them about these issues. Then we offer the boss a graceful retreat— that we are very busy right now. The response will usually be something like this: "Oh, never mind. Project X is important and you should focus on that. We can find someone else to attend the meeting."

In general, this tactic is to first agree, then suggest we will do something damaging to the organization's interests, and finally give the requestor an easy way to retract the request. It usually works quite well, but if it does not, or if we are not interested in appearing to be a dissenter, then we will have to attend the meeting. In such cases, there are some other zero-planning tactics we can employ.

First of all, we are still in command of our poise, confidence, and dignity. So we are not going to get shaken by whatever transpires. We will simply enjoy it, do our best to generate comfort and enjoyment, and not get too worried about the whole thing.

Second, we can use our unfamiliarity to our advantage. Almost everyone enjoys talking about their own particular interests, so we rely more heavily on questioning techniques than we would had we been given time to prepare. It is usually pretty easy to get a group talking about their endeavors and challenges to an attentive listener. So we assume that role and pay careful attention, doing all the information-gathering we can in this short time span. We have to be careful here, as it is not good to give the impression that we are stalling or trying to turn the meeting in our own direction. However, a few questions will often generate some lively discussion, and give us some ammunition for engaging the group. We simply will not have the time to organize our thoughts as well as we would if we had been able to glean this information ahead of time. Just remember that we are working with precious little information anyway (that's why it is called an *unfamiliar* group). So having less information than very little information is not really a severe handicap.

In summary, meeting with an unfamiliar group is not such a big deal. We know how to prepare, generate comfort, and make the whole thing enjoyable for all. We also have learned some techniques for zero-preparation situations, not the least of which is another meeting-avoidance technique, which is always an asset. Most importantly, we see that having no preparation time for meeting with an unfamiliar group is not so far removed from having lots of time, so we do not need to worry too much about it.

14

CONCLUSION

Now that you have read the whole book, I want to leave you with a few simple thoughts. For any communication event, whether for a familiar or unfamiliar audience or group of readers:

In Planning	Focus on connection, flow, and reinforcement.
In Attitude	Have fun, strive to please readers, and attend to their needs, but remain indifferent to audiences and meeting participants, and maintain your self-esteem.
In Execution	Isolate yourself when writing; be poised, dignified, and confident when presenting or interacting; and don't worry about the outcomes.
In Tools	Use simple, effective ones.
In Trouble?	Because you applied the principles I recommended to compensate for zero-time demands too vigorously and angered those you work for? Who cares? Go work for some reasonable folks, or freelance.

I hope you enjoyed reading this little book as much as I enjoyed writing it. Adding Part IV for this new edition was a lot of fun. Now you are ready to use these concepts and techniques for more enjoyable and effective communication. Good luck!

INDEX

I didn't think we really needed an index. Besides, going through all the material in the book and trying to decide what should or shouldn't be in the index is a lot of trouble. This is a *little* book. To find a topic of interest, all you need to do is look over the contents, figure out which chapter the topic is likely to be in, and browse through the chapter until you find it. If you find something else useful along the way, so much the better. If you have to read the whole chapter to find it, so what? What's the rush? No chapter is more than a few pages, and from reading this book in the first place, you understand the value of not being in such a big hurry all the time.

However, the publisher said, "Yes, we do need an index." Furthermore, the publishing industry at large seems to consider books without indexes pretty useless. With these kind of pressures brought to bear, I naturally agreed to provide an index, and here it is.

INDEX

INDEX

INDEX

About the Author

Herbert L. Hirsch is a senior consulting engineer with a B.S. in electrical engineering from the University of Cincinnati. He has 30 years' experience designing electronic systems, system and phenomenology simulations, and signal/image processing algorithms primarily for military sensor systems. He developed the communication techniques described in this book in the course of preparing hundreds of technical documents, presentations, and proposals during his engineering career.

Mr. Hirsch began his career at Systems Research Laboratories (now part of Veridian Corp.) in Dayton, Ohio, where he held engineer and senior engineer positions. He was an engineering group leader for Quest Research Corporation, the director of systems engineering for Applications Research Corporation, the director of engineering for Defense Technology, Inc., and chief engineer for MTL Systems, Inc.—all in Dayton, Ohio. He currently operates his consulting business, Hirsch Engineering and Communications, Inc., from his home in Vandalia, Ohio.

Mr. Hirsch has published or copublished numerous books on communication, radar antenna simulation, statistical signal processing, hardware description languages, and electronic countermeasures, including *The Essence of Technical Communication for Engineers* (IEEE Press, 2000), *Effective Design and Testing with WAVES and VHDL* (Kluwer Academic Publishers, 1996), Chapter 11 in *The CM Handbook for Aircraft Survivability* (USAF, 1994), *Statistical Signal Characterization* (Artech House, 1991), and *Practical Simulation of Radar Antennas and Radomes* (Artech House, 1988).